MAIN   MAR 09 2007

578 .77 WAL
Walker, Pam, 1958-
The continental shelf /

D1501561

PALM BEACH COUNTY
LIBRARY SYSTEM
3650 SUMMIT BLVD.
WEST PALM BEACH, FL 33406

The Continental Shelf

Life in the Sea

The Continental Shelf

Pam Walker and
Elaine Wood

Facts On File, Inc.

The Continental Shelf

Copyright © 2005 by Pam Walker and Elaine Wood

All rights reserved. No part of this book may be reproduced or utilized in any form or by any means, electronic or mechanical, including photocopying, recording, or by any information storage or retrieval systems, without permission in writing from the publisher. For information contact:

Facts On File, Inc.
132 West 31st Street
New York NY 10001

Library of Congress Cataloging-in-Publication Data
Walker, Pam, 1958–
The continental shelf/ Pam Walker and Elaine Wood.
p. cm. — (Life in the sea)
Includes bibliographical references and index.
ISBN 0-8160-5704-4 (hardcover)
1. Marine biology—Juvenile literature. 2. Continental shelf—
Juvenile literature. I. Wood, Elaine, 1950– II. Title.
QH541.5.S3W36 2005
578.77—dc22   2004024226

Facts On File books are available at special discounts when purchased in bulk quantities for businesses, associations, institutions, or sales promotions. Please call our Special Sales Department in New York at
(212) 967-8800 or (800) 322-8755.

You can find Facts On File on the World Wide Web at
http://www.factsonfile.com

Text and cover design by Dorothy M. Preston
Illustrations by Dale Williams, Sholto Ainslie, and Dale Dyer

Printed in the United States of America

VB FOF 10 9 8 7 6 5 4 3 2 1

This book is printed on acid-free paper.

Contents

Preface

*L*ife first appeared on Earth in the oceans, about 3.5 billion years ago. Today these immense bodies of water still hold the greatest diversity of living things on the planet. The sheer size and wealth of the oceans are startling. They cover two-thirds of the Earth's surface and make up the largest habitat in this solar system. This immense underwater world is a fascinating realm that captures the imaginations of people everywhere.

Even though the sea is a powerful and immense system, people love it. Nationwide, more than half of the population lives near one of the coasts, and the popularity of the seashore as a home or place of recreation continues to grow. Increasing interest in the sea environment and the singular organisms it conceals is swelling the ranks of marine aquarium hobbyists, scuba divers, and deep-sea fishermen. In schools and universities across the United States, marine science is working its way into the science curriculum as one of the foundation sciences.

The purpose of this book is to foster the natural fascination that people feel for the ocean and its living things. As a part of the set entitled Life in the Sea, this book aims to give readers a glimpse of some of the wonders of life that are hidden beneath the waves and to raise awareness of the relationships that people around the world have with the ocean.

This book also presents an opportunity to consider the ways that humans affect the oceans. At no time in the past have world citizens been so poised to impact the future of the planet. Once considered an endless and resilient resource, the ocean is now being recognized as a fragile system in danger of overuse and neglect. As knowledge and understanding about the ocean's importance grow, citizens all over the world can participate in positively changing the ways that life on land interacts with life in the sea.

Acknowledgments

$\mathcal{T}$his opportunity to study and research ocean life has reminded both of us of our past love affairs with the sea. Like many families, ours took annual summer jaunts to the beach, where we got our earliest gulps of salt water and fingered our first sand dollars. As sea-loving children, both of us grew into young women who aspired to be marine biologists, dreaming of exciting careers spent nursing wounded seals, surveying the dark abyss, or discovering previously unknown species. After years of teaching school, these dreams gave way to the reality that we would not spend our careers working with sea creatures, as we had hoped. But time and distance never diminished our love and respect for the oceans and their residents.

We are thrilled to have the chance to use our own experiences and appreciation of the sea as platforms from which to develop these books on ocean life. Our thanks go to Frank K. Darmstadt, executive editor at Facts On File, for this enjoyable opportunity. He has guided us through the process with patience, which we greatly appreciate. Frank's skills are responsible for the book's tone and focus. Our appreciation also goes to Katy Barnhart for her copyediting expertise.

Special notes of appreciation go to several individuals whose expertise made this book possible. Audrey McGhee proofread and corrected pages at all times of the day or night. Diane Kit Moser, Ray Spangenburg, and Bobbi McCutcheon, successful and seasoned authors, mentored us on techniques for finding appropriate photographs. We appreciate the help of these generous and talented people.

Introduction

*T*he waters where surfers dare the waves and commercial fishermen earn their livings are components of the nearshore regions of the ocean known as the continental shelves. Covered by water that varies from knee deep to depths of 656.2 feet (200 m), the continental shelves are the flat, submerged edges of the landmasses. Shelf waters are rich in nutrients, which they receive from both the open ocean and the land. For this reason, marine environments on the continental shelves are able to support dense populations of living things.

The Continental Shelf is one volume in Facts On File's Life in the Sea, a set of six texts that examine the physical features and biology of different regions of the ocean. Chapter 1 explores the features of the seafloor and the water column that make these marine environments unique. Because the Sun provides the energy for living things, the degree to which light penetrates water has a tremendous impact on the kinds of organisms that make their homes there, and explains why the deeper regions of the shelf have no plant life. Other factors that delineate these nearshore environments include the saltiness and amount of oxygen dissolved in water, temperature, and the types of substrates on the seafloor. In oceans, the greatest percentage of living things is found just above, or within, the sediments. Depending on geographical location, sediments vary from sandy to rocky, and include soil from the land as well as the shells and external skeletons of billions of tiny marine creatures.

Continental shelf food chains, especially their beginnings and ends, make up the subject matter of chapter 2. As in all food chains, life on the continental shelf is supported by the work of producers. In shallow shelf waters, light reaches the seafloor, where it maintains grassy meadows and forest of sea-weeds, including the red, green, and brown algae. The rich supply of nutrients in the water also provides food for dense populations of microscopic green organisms.

In low-oxygen muds of the shelf, single-celled bacteria that can derive energy from chemicals make their homes. Bacteria that decompose organic matter are also abundant on the substrates of shelf waters, where they play roles in recycling key nutrients through the ecosystems.

Simple animals like sponges, jellyfish, and worms are the topic of chapter 3. Sponges display a variety of shapes and colors, depending on their location and the degree to which they are exposed to the action of waves. Shallow water sponges form crusts over rocks and the shells of hermit crabs and other animals. Those that live in deeper water, like the red strawberry sponge or the iridescent tube sponge, grow tall, forming structures that resemble tubes, urns, and fingers. Glass sponges build extensive reefs in deep shelf waters, where they provide habitats for hundreds of other kinds of animals. Cnidarians in shelf waters include tube anemones and daisy anemones, small animals that attach to the substrate, as well as reef-building corals like common brain coral and *Oculina*. Hundreds of species of jellyfish are common, like the beautiful purple-striped jellyfish and the stinging sea nettle. Worms in the region vary from the tissue-thin candy-striped flatworm to the secretive, tube-dwelling bamboo worm that feeds by extending antennae above the soil.

Advanced animals like mollusks, crustaceans, echinoderms, and tunicates, discussed in chapter 4, are numerous in shelf waters. Flat-shelled abalone and large, slow-moving queen conch live on the seafloor, sharing space with the Pacific littleneck clam, the blue clam, and the great scallop. A variety of sea stars feed on the clams and mussels, prying their shells open with their strong tube feet. Crawling over and among these slow animals are the common octopus, the red octopus and the giant octopus, all accomplished predators. The upper levels of water contain animals of all sorts, including krill, small shrimplike organisms that serve as the primary source of food for many whales as well as fish and sea birds.

Chapter 5 looks at some of the many kinds of fish that live in continental shelf waters, including the swimming species like tuna and mackerel as well as those that spend most of their lives hiding in the sediments, such as flounder and sole. Fish that swim close to the seafloor, the bony groundfish, include cod and pollock, important commercial species. Not as numerous, but still important to the ecosystems they inhabit, are the fish whose skeletons are made of cartilage instead of bone, the skates, rays, and sharks. The big skates, Southern stingrays, and graceful rays swim near the bottom, pausing occasionally to stir up sediments with a flapping motion that helps them uncover prey. Dogfish and horned sharks are predators that patrol continental shelf waters, while the much larger basking and whale sharks feed on microscopic organisms that they filter from the water column.

The reptiles, birds, and mammals of the continental shelf are some of the most visible, and best known, inhabitants, and are the subjects of chapter 6. Five species of sea turtles spend some, or all, of their time in waters of the continental shelves: the Atlantic leatherback, the Atlantic loggerhead, Ridley's sea turtle, the Atlantic hawksbill, and the green sea turtle. All five groups of turtles are endangered, and their populations are small. Seabirds are a much larger group and include the penguins, auks, shearwaters, petrels, boobies, cormorants, frigatebirds, and jaegers. Each type of bird is highly specialized for life at sea. Penguins do not fly, using their wings as flippers for swimming, but the wings of auks are adapted for both flying and swimming. Shearwaters and fulmars pluck small fish and crustaceans from the water's surface, while boobies dive into the water and pursue their prey. Marine mammals that make their homes in shelf waters include otters, seals, whales, dugongs, and manatees. Whales are subdivided into two groups: the baleen whales and the toothed whales, which include beaked dolphins and porpoises. Baleen whales feed by filtering tiny organisms through sievelike plates of baleen, while toothed whales are carnivores that hunt and kill their food.

Because the continental shelves border land and are easily accessible to humans, they suffer from pollution, overfishing, and other problems. Recognition of these problems is the first step toward remediating the damage already done. Several continental shelf environments receive special protection, such as coral reefs, kelp beds, and sea grass meadows. By preserving these fragile marine environments, people ensure that they will be intact for the next generation.

Physical Aspects
Origins, Science, and Processes of Continental Shelf Environments

*T*he Earth can be described as the "water world" because more than 70 percent of its surface is covered in water. The remaining 30 percent of the planet is made up of continents. Even though coastlines mark the visible boundaries between the land and the sea, the continents do not really end at the coasts. They extend underwater well past the point where the ocean laps up on the shores. These submerged edges of the continents are called the continental margins.

Worldwide, continental margins are only a small portion of the ocean, making up a mere 8 percent of the surface and only 0.2 percent of the total volume. These narrow bands of relatively shallow water are such productive areas that they support more life forms than the rest of the open seas. A full 99 percent of the ocean's fish make their homes along the continental margins.

The continental margins owe their high productivity to their locations. Nutrients derived from the land are carried by waterways to the coast, where they empty into the sea along the continental margins. Most of the nutrients remain in shallow coastal waters, but strong currents sweep some farther out into the deeper waters near the continental margins.

Humans have always valued the waters of continental margins. These are the places where the world's commercial fishermen, as well as recreational sportsmen, harvest their catches. Shelf waters are close to shores, so they serve as routes to seaports all around the world. As a result, waters of the continental margins are constantly impacted by people.

Features of the Ocean Floor

The structure of continental margins can best be understood by examining the geologic history of the Earth. The continents and seas have not always been in their present positions. In fact, these enormous bodies have been slowly shifting since Earth's earliest days. The mechanism that moves these immense geologic structures, plate tectonics, gets its energy from the center of the Earth.

The Earth is made of three basic layers: the core, mantle, and crust. The core, which is the densest and hottest layer, is located at the center of the Earth. Outside the core is the mantle, a cooler and less dense layer. Nearest the core, the mantle is very dense and thick, but the outermost section, the athenosphere, exists in the molten lava state.

On top of the mantle is the lithosphere, or crust, the thinnest layer. The crust is not homogenous but is made of two very different kinds of materials: the oceanic crust and the continental crust. The oceanic crust, the part that stretches under the oceans, is a very thin layer of dense minerals that is only four miles (6.4 km) deep. The continental crust, which makes up all of the continents, is composed of less dense matter and is thicker, averaging 25 to 30 miles (40.2 to 48.3 km) deep.

The two kinds of crusts form seven gigantic plates that float on top of the mantle. Each of these plates interlocks with those surrounding it, very much like the parts of a puzzle. These seven pieces of crust are named for their locations and include the Pacific, Eurasian, African, Australian, North American, South American, and Antarctic plates. Each plate includes portions of both continental and oceanic crust.

Beneath the crust, the molten section of the mantle moves slowly in huge, circular currents. This movement is created by variations in density in different parts of the mantle. Dense regions of molten material slowly sink, and less dense areas rise, creating continuous convection currents.

In a few locations, molten material gets close enough to the surface of the Earth to push up through the crust and spill out in the form of volcanoes. One area of the world where magma often surfaces is at the midoceanic ridge. Magma extruded at the midoceanic ridge creates an extensive range of undersea mountains in the Atlantic Ocean. Molten rock that wells to the surface separates the two sides of the ridge. As the ridge widens, each side pushes portions of oceanic crust ahead of it.

The addition of new crust widens the floor of the Atlantic Ocean. This phenomenon, which is known as seafloor spreading, constantly moves the Americas farther from Europe and Africa.

Plates that are pushed ahead of new crust must have somewhere to go. On their leading edges, many of them are forced down under, or subducted beneath, other plates. In many of the regions where crust is subducted, deep ocean trenches form. Once pressed down into the hot mantle, the old crust liquefies. At other places, two plates may push past one another along big cracks or breaks in the crust known as faults. All this movement of plates as a result of seafloor spreading is called continental drift.

Over the Earth's history, continental drift and seafloor spreading have created mountains, valleys, trenches, and canyons in the oceans as well as on the continents. Although most people are familiar with the geology of continents, some of the most dramatic geologic forms are out of sight deep in the sea. Scientists have created a generalized map of the ocean floor that includes many of the undersea geologic features. The region of seafloor nearest the coast is the continental margin. As shown in Figure 1.1, the continental margin is made up of three sections: the continental shelf, the continental slope, and the continental rise.

The continental shelves are shallow-water areas when compared to the rest of the oceans. These generally flat expanses average 40 miles (68 km) wide, although they vary tremendously. For example, the continental shelf along some parts of the African and North American coasts is almost nonexistent, while on the coast of Siberia it is 930 miles (1,500 km) wide. Depths of continental shelf waters average 430 feet (130 m) but range from a few inches to 1,800 feet (550 m). Continental shelves are covered in deep layers of sediment that have washed onto them from adjoining landmasses.

A steep drop-off marks the outermost edge of the shelf and the beginning of the continental slope. In some regions, the slope is a sharp one, and depth increases rapidly, finally leveling off at about 11,811 feet (3,600 m). The slope is scarred with occasional V-shaped submarine canyons, many of which

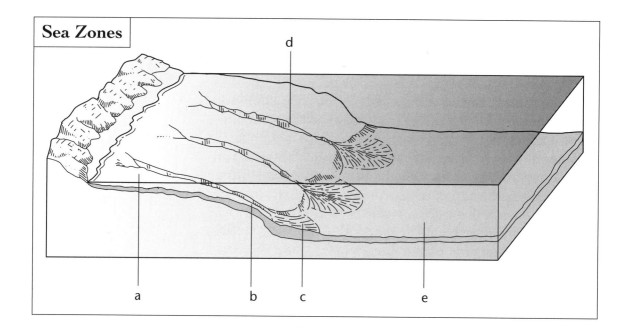

Sea Zones

d

a   b   c   e

Fig. 1.1 The continental shelf (a) begins a downward slant at the continental slope (b). At the foot of the slope is the continental rise (c). Submarine canyons (d) can be found in some continental slopes. Extending seaward from the continental rise is the abyssal plain (e).

were carved by rivers at a time when the oceans' water levels were lower and the shelves were exposed.

A pile of sediment at the base of each continental slope is called the continental rise. This mound was created by processes like undersea landslides that carried materials from the shelf to the foot of the slope. Continental rises are common in the Atlantic and Indian Oceans, but rare in the Pacific Ocean. In the Pacific, the bases of many continental slopes border trenches.

Other ocean floor features include volcanic mountains, deep-sea trenches, wide abyssal plains, abyssal hills, and seamounts, steep-sided, underwater mountains that were formed by volcanic activity. In addition, volcanic mountains are found in every ocean. Deep-sea trenches, like the Pacific's Marianas Trench and the Atlantic's Sandwich Trench, are the deepest points in the ocean.

Zones in the Ocean

When viewed from the land, ocean waters appear to be wide, homogeneous expanses with wavy surfaces. Nothing could be further from the truth. Concealed beneath the oceans' waves are thousands of unique habitats and niches, each the result of one-of-a-kind combinations of light, temperature, water chemistry, and nutrients. Ocean habitats are found in the water column and on the seafloor. For convenience, both the water and the ocean floor are divided into zones.

Water above the deep ocean floor is called the pelagic or oceanic zone, whereas that over the shallower continental shelf is described as the neritic zone or nearshore water. The region below the water is the seafloor, or the benthos. Water above the seafloor is divided into regions by depth. Starting at the high tide mark and moving out to sea, these regions include the intertidal, sublittoral, bathyal, abyssal, and hadal zones.

The intertidal zone is the stretch of ocean between high and low tides. This area of shallow, tidal water is only found along the coasts. The sublittoral zone, the section of seafloor beneath neritic waters, begins at the base of the intertidal zone and extends across the width of continental shelves. Consequently, sublittoral substrates exist from depths of just a few inches to 656.2 feet (200 m). The sublittoral zone ends at the point where the continental shelf begins its sharp, downward descent.

The bathyal zone starts at the continental slope and includes the slope as well as the continental rise, a section of floor where water varies in depth from 656.2 feet (200 m) to 6,561.7 feet (2,000 m). Past the continental rise are the deepest sections of the sea: the abyssal zone, whose depths extend from 6,561.7 to 19,685 feet (2,000 to 6,000 m), and the hadal zone, which includes water that reaches depths of 36,089.2 feet (11,000 m).

Science of Continental Shelf Waters

For living things, the seafloor is a critically important part of the marine environment. The floor provides the substrate on which 98 percent of the marine organisms live. Most of these organisms are found within the boundaries of continental shelves where water is relatively shallow and nutrients are plentiful.

The seafloor of the continental shelf is not uniform. Soft substrate covers most areas, although some regions are rocky and others are bare. Soft sediments make good homes for burrowing organisms as well as those that lie on top of the seafloor. Rocks and hard sediments provide ideal substrates for organisms that need a place to attach. In well-lit zones, grasses and macroalgae like kelp attach to firm materials on the floor.

Sediments that cover the floor of the continental shelf were derived from four kinds of sources: the land, the sea, living organisms, and the atmosphere. Those from the land, the terrigenous sediments, result from the erosive actions of wind, rain, and ice on soil and rocks. Much of the clay that makes its way to the ocean is transported there by rivers that drain the continents, but some also travels there on the wind. Clay is the smallest and lightest type of soil particle. When a wind-blown bit of clay settles into the ocean, it may stay suspended in the water for several years before finally sinking all the way to the bottom.

Sediments derived from living organisms, biogenous materials, are made up of the hard body parts of animals. Biogenous sediments include crushed limestone shells, like those from snails and clams. In addition, the outer body coverings of microscopic organisms, such as diatoms, coccolithophores, and foraminifera, also find their way to the seafloor.

Certain chemical reactions in seawater produce insoluble materials, or precipitates, such as calcium compounds and carbonates. These materials may stay suspended in the water column for a while but eventually settle to the bottom.

One type of seafloor sediment enters the water from the atmosphere, but originates from outer space. When a particle traveling through space hits the water, it either dissolves or drifts for a time before settling to the bottom. The majority of outer space particles are tiny, but they are rich in iron and act as a source of this important mineral for some marine organisms.

Salinity, Temperature, and Density

Although marine environments can be characterized by their substrates, they are also defined by other qualities. Physical and chemical characteristics of water, including factors such as *salinity,* levels of dissolved gases, density, and temperature, influence marine environments. Each factor helps determine what kinds of organisms can make their homes there.

The amount of dissolved minerals, or salts, in ocean water is referred to as the water's salinity. On the average, salinity of ocean water is about 35 parts of salt to 1,000 parts of water. Salinity is not constant throughout the oceans; it is much lower in places where freshwater enters, such as near the mouth of a river. Salinity tends to be high in regions where the climate is hot and dry. In such climates, water evaporates quickly, leaving behind its dissolved salts.

Like sediments, the dissolved minerals that make up sea salts come from land. Weathering slowly breaks down soil and rocks into ions, or charged particles, which travel to the ocean in the waters of creeks and rivers. Most of the dissolved minerals in water are salts made from sodium and chloride ions. Some of the other ions that find their way to the ocean are sulfate, magnesium, calcium, and potassium.

The chemical composition of seawater has remained relatively constant for the last 1.5 billion years, despite the fact that ions of various kinds are constantly added to the ocean. Ions do not accumulate in the ocean because several mechanisms remove them from the system as quickly as they are deposited. Many ions stick to sediments that slowly drift through the water column and eventually settle on the seafloor, where they are effectively removed from the water column. Others are taken out of ocean water by chemical reactions in the sea that convert some of the dissolved minerals into insoluble compounds. These, too, accumulate on the bottom of the ocean. Salt is also lost from ocean waters when waves strike the shore, spraying fine mists of salt-laden water on rocks, plants, and other seaside objects. In addition, in some areas, seawater gets trapped in small shallow ponds; when water evaporates from these ponds, the minerals are left behind.

Just as there are gases in the atmosphere surrounding the Earth, there are also gases in its water. Living things in both terrestrial and aquatic environments require oxygen, carbon dioxide, and other gases to survive. Gases in the atmosphere dissolve in water, where they become available to aquatic life forms.

Chemical and Physical Characteristics of Water

Water is one of the most wide-spread materials on this planet. Water fills the oceans, sculpts the land, and is a primary component in all living things. For all of its commonness, water is a very unusual molecule whose unique qualities are due to its physical structure.

Water is a compound made up of three atoms: two hydrogen atoms and one oxygen atom. The way these three atoms bond causes one end of the resulting molecule to have a slightly negative charge, and the other end a slightly positive charge. For this reason water is described as a polar molecule.

The positive end of one water molecule is attracted to the negative end of another water molecule. When two oppositely charged ends of water molecules get close enough to each other, a bond forms between them. This kind of bond is a hydrogen bond. Every water molecule can form hydrogen bonds with other water molecules. Even though hydrogen bonds are weaker than the bonds that hold together the atoms within a water molecule, they are strong enough to affect the nature of water and give this unusual liquid some unique characteristics.

Water is the only substance on Earth that exists in all three states of matter: solid, liquid, and gas. Because hydrogen bonds are relatively strong, a lot of energy is needed to separate water molecules from one another. That is why water can absorb more heat than any other material before its temperature increases and before it changes from one state to another.

Since water molecules stick to one another, liquid water has a lot of surface tension. Surface tension is a measure of how easy or difficult it is to break the surface of a liquid. These hydrogen bonds give water's surface a weak, membranelike quality that affects the way water forms waves and currents. The surface tension of water also impacts the organisms that live in the water column, water below the surface, as well as those on its surface.

Atmospheric gases, such as oxygen and carbon dioxide, are capable of dissolving in water, but not all gases dissolve with the same ease. Carbon dioxide dissolves more easily than oxygen, and there is always plenty of carbon dioxide in seawater. On the other hand, water holds only $\frac{1}{100}$ the volume of oxygen found in the atmosphere. Low oxygen levels in water can limit the number and types of organisms that live there. The concentration of dissolved gases is affected by temperature. Gases dissolve more easily in cold water than in warm, so cold water is richer in oxygen and carbon dioxide than warm water. Gases are also more likely to dissolve in shallow water than deep. In shallow water, oxygen gas from the atmosphere is mixed with water by winds and waves. In addition, plants, which produce oxygen gas in the process of photosynthesis, are found in shallow water.

Water Molecules

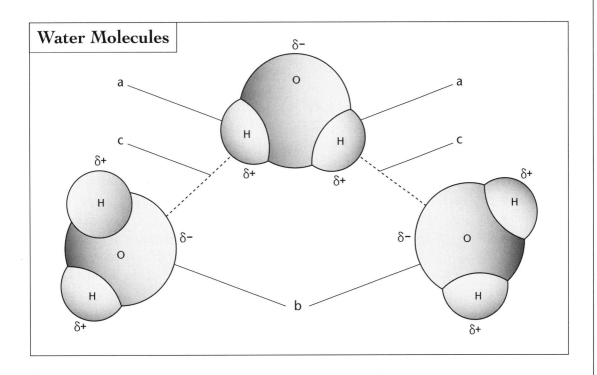

Fig. 1.2   A water molecule is made up of two hydrogen atoms (a) bonded to one oxygen atom (b). The large nucleus of the oxygen atom causes the electrons in the resulting molecule to spend more time near the oxygen end of the molecule than near the hydrogen ends. Therefore, the oxygen end has a slightly negative charge δ^- and the hydrogen ends have slightly positive charges δ^+. The slightly positive end of one water molecule is attracted to the slightly negative end of another water molecule, creating a hydrogen bond (c) between the two molecules.

The temperature of seawater is critically important to the organisms that live in it. Temperature, a measure of the amount of heat in a system, affects the rates at which chemical reactions occur. Up to a point, as temperature increases, reaction rates increase. As a result, many warm water species of organisms have faster rates of metabolism, the chemical reactions of their bodies, than similar forms that live in cold water. Consequently, organisms tend to grow faster, and larger, in the tropics than they do near the poles.

Geographic location, water depth, and the seasons impact the temperatures of waters. On the average, water in the oceans is cold, hovering only a few degrees above freezing. The warmest marine waters are those at the surface in shallow coastal areas and in the tropics. The coolest are found in the open ocean, the deep ocean, and near the poles.

The properties of temperature and salinity affect the density of seawater. Density is a measurement of matter's mass per unit volume. Seawater is denser than freshwater because seawater contains more dissolved minerals than fresh. As the salinity of water increases, so does its density.

Temperature impacts the density of water because of its effects on water's volume. Generally, as temperature increases, water expands and takes up more space. A mass of warm water has a greater volume that a mass of the same amount of cool water. As a result, warm water has a lower density than cool water.

Density is an important factor in seawater because it determines where water will be located in the water column, the vast region from surface to seafloor. Since dense water sinks below less dense water, both very salty and extremely cold water move to the lowest level of a water column. Cold, salty water is the densest kind, whereas warm salt water diluted by freshwater is the least dense.

Light in Continental Shelf Waters

The majority of sea organisms depend on the Sun to provide them with energy. Sunlight must be present for photosynthesis to occur. During photosynthesis, green organisms convert

How Light Penetrates Water

Light is a form of energy that travels in waves. When the Sun's light arrives at Earth, it has a white quality to it. As shown in Figure 1.3, white light is made up of the colors of the rainbow: violet, indigo, blue, green, yellow, orange, and red. The color of light is dependent on the length of the light wave. Light in the visible spectrum includes the colors that people can see, light whose wavelengths vary between 0.4 and 0.8 microns. (A micron is one one-millionth of a meter.) Violet light has the shortest wavelength in the visible spectrum and red has the longest.

Light is affected differently by water than it is by air. Air transmits light, but water can transmit, absorb, and reflect light, depending on its depth and contents. The fact that water transmits light makes it possible for photosynthesis to take place under water. However, all of the wavelengths of visible light do not penetrate the same depth. Blue light penetrates the most and red light the least. For that reason, if water is very clear, blue light penetrates it deeply and gives the water a blue color.

Light on the red side of the spectrum is quickly absorbed as heat, so red only penetrates to 49.2 feet (15 m). That is why water at the ocean's surface is warmer than deep water. Green light, in the middle of the spectrum, reaches greater depths; it is often reflected back from particles that are suspended in the middle range of the water column. Water that contains a lot of suspended particles, such as soil or plant matter, has a greenish brown hue.

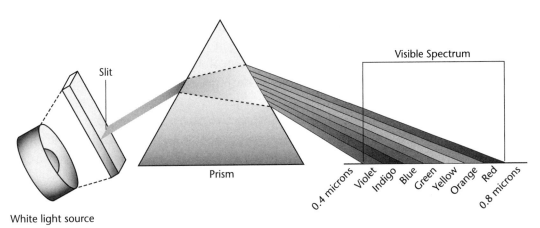

Fig. 1.3 Light in the visible spectrum has a white quality but is actually made up of colors. Color is dependent on wavelength; violet has the shortest wavelength, and red has the longest.

carbon dioxide and water into energy and oxygen. Since one of the raw materials of photosynthesis is carbon dioxide, and one of the by-products is oxygen, the rate at which this reaction occurs also affects levels of these two dissolved gases.

Sea plants and land plants are not exposed to the same amount of sunlight. Plants growing on the land are flooded with light, which easily penetrates the air. Water limits the depth to which light can penetrate. Therefore plants in water receive much less light than their terrestrial counterparts.

Neritic waters, those over the continental margins, can be divided into three zones based on the depth of light penetration: photic, dysphotic, and aphotic. The uppermost part of the water makes up the photic zone, the area where there is enough light for photosynthesis to take place. The depth of the photic zone varies from 65.6 feet (20 m) to 328.1 feet (100 m), depending on the clarity of the water. Below that is the dysphotic zone, the area where light is too weak for photosynthesis to occur. Also known as the twilight zone, this region receives only 5 percent of the sunlight that strikes the surface. Depending on clarity, the dysphotic zone varies in depth from 328.1 feet (100 m) to 656.2 feet (200 m). Below the dysphotic zone is the aphotic zone, where no light penetrates.

Tides, Waves, Winds, and Currents

In the ocean, the position of a water sample in the water column depends on physical factors such as salinity, temperature, and density. The layer of water at the top of the water column, from the surface down to 330 feet (100 m), is warmed by heat from the Sun and mixed by the energy of winds. Beneath the surface water, extending from 330 feet (100 m) to 3,300 feet (1,000 m), the temperature of water decreases and its salinity increases. As a result, the density of water increases with depth, until 3,300 feet (1,000 m). At this point, the temperature, salinity, and density of water rarely change.

During cool weather, water forms strata in which upper layers are less dense than lower ones. In this arrangement, water is stable and experiences very little movement. In warm weather, evaporation of water from the surface increases the

Tides

Tides result from a combination of three forces: the gravitational force of the Sun, the gravitational force of the Moon, and the motion of the Earth. Gravity is the force of attraction, or pull, between two bodies. Everything that has mass exerts gravity. The Earth and Moon exert gravitational pulls on each other. Because the Earth has more mass than the Moon, its gravity keeps the Moon in orbit. The Moon does not fall into the Earth because of the inertia, the tendency of a moving object to keep moving, that is created by their stable orbits.

The inward force of gravity and the outward force of inertia affect the entire surface of the Earth, but not to the same degree. Owing to Earth's rounded shape, the equator is closer to the Moon than Earth's poles are. The pull of the Moon's gravity is consequently stronger around the equator. On the side of the Earth facing the Moon at any given time, the Moon's gravity pulls the Earth toward it. The solid Earth is unable to respond dramatically to that pull, but the liquid part of Earth can. As a result, the ocean bulges out toward the Moon on the side of Earth that is facing it. On the side that is farthest from the Moon, inertia flings water away from the Moon. The Moon's pull on one side of Earth and the force of inertia on the opposite side create two bulges—high tides—in the ocean.

The bulges do not rotate around the Earth as it turns on its axis. Instead, they remain aligned with the Moon as the Earth rotates under them. Different parts of the Earth move into and out of these bulges as it goes through one rotation, or one day.

Even though the Sun is much farther from Earth than the Moon is, the Sun also has an effect on tides. The Sun's influence is only about half that of the Moon's. A small solar bulge on Earth follows the Sun throughout the day, and the side of the Earth opposite the Sun experiences a small inertial bulge.

The Moon revolves around the Earth in a 28-day cycle. As it does so, the positions of the Moon, Earth, and Sun relative to one another change. The three bodies are perfectly aligned during two phases: new moon and full moon. At these times, the Sun and Moon forces are acting on the same area of Earth at the same time, causing high tide to be at its highest and low tide to be at its lowest. These extremes are known as spring tides and occur every two weeks.

During first- and third-quarter conditions, when only one-half of the Moon is visible in the night sky, the Sun and Moon are at right angles to the Earth. In these positions, their gravitational pulls are working against each other, and the two bodies cancel each other's effects to some degree, causing high tides to be at their lowest, and low tides to be at their highest. These neap tides also occur every two weeks.

density of the upper layer. When density is higher in the upper levels than in the lower ones, the water column becomes unstable. Dense water sinks and the less dense water rises, causing the column of water to mix from top to bottom. Regions of sinking, dense water are known as downwelling zones. Downwellings can be good for the immediate marine environment because they carry oxygen-rich water from the surface to the depths, where oxygen levels are often low.

Regions where water at the bottom of the water column moves to the surface are called upwelling zones. Upwellings bring nutrients to the surface of the water, where they become available to organisms such as one-celled algae. In water that does not experience upwelling, organic matter and nutrients tend to collect in the sediment where they are isolated from living things.

Other processes that move water are tides, winds, and currents. Tides are the regular rising and falling of large bodies of water. Even though tides affect the entire ocean, they are more obvious in the relatively shallow waters over the continental shelf than they are in the deep ocean.

Wind blowing across the surface of the water creates waves and currents. A wave is a ridge of water that seems to be traveling across the ocean's surface. Water does not really travel in a wave. The only thing that travels in a wave is energy; the water simply moves up and down. Waves can also be started by energy from sources such as landslides, volcanic eruptions, and movements along faults on the ocean floor.

Water moves from one area of the ocean to another in big streams or currents. Winds create the currents near the water's surface, so many ocean currents follow the same paths as wind belts. There are dozens of ocean currents, all named for their positions on the Earth. The Gulf Stream is a current that flows northward along the eastern coast of North America, carrying warm tropical water with it. The California Current flows southward along the western coast, moving cold water from the north Pacific toward the equator.

The energy of tides, waves, and currents affects the conditions on the seafloor and the organisms that live there. Depending on conditions, energy can churn the bottom sediments of both shallow and deep ocean waters, often making it difficult for organisms to settle or attach. In regions of the ocean that are protected from tides, waves, and currents, levels of energy are low. These low-energy sites provide good homes for life forms that cannot tolerate shifting conditions.

Energy affects the type and size of particles that make up the sediment. In many near-shore areas where energy is high, large soil particles such as sand and gravel accumulate. Such materials support animals like clams and sponges that filter or strain their food from the water. Low-energy areas tend to be covered with small particles such as mud-forming clays. As a result, they provide ideal environments for worms, crabs, and other animals that sift their food out of the substrate.

Habitats

Continental shelves provide thousands of different habitats, or places for organisms to live. Habitats are influenced by the geological, chemical, and physical features of the continental margins and the waters over them. Some of the habitats that are found on the continental margins include soft bottom, sea grass, hard substrate, kelp, and coral reef.

Soft substrates may make up more than 50 percent of the continental shelf floor. In these areas, sand, silt, mud, and dead organic matter compose the sediments. In some places the soft bottoms are covered with colonies of green one-celled organisms. In others, soft bottoms contain rotting plant parts and other dead organic matter that was delivered to the shelves by the action of rivers. Both the green cells and the decaying matter provide food for organisms that live burrowed in the sediment and for those lying on top of it. In soft sediment regions, populations of organisms are not evenly distributed. They occur in patches around clumps of nutrients.

Some soft bottom areas develop stands of sea grasses, which have a stabilizing effect on the seabed. The extensive root systems of grasses enable them to stay in place when buffeted by strong waves or currents. Blades of sea grasses slow down the movement of water, causing it to deposit some of its load of suspended material. The accumulation of suspended matter and sediment around the plants helps build up soil in soft bottom communities.

Sea grass beds, which are more common in the tropics than in temperate zones, provide other benefits. They are important habitats for young organisms, providing them with places to hide and feed. In addition, sea grass beds physically support several species of plants and animals that live on the grass fronds. Plants that reside on other organisms, like sea grass, are collectively known as epiphytes. Epizooics are animals that live on other organisms. In many sea grass meadows, the populations of epiphytes and epizooics exceed the population of sea grasses that support them.

Very few grazing animals eat the standing crop, the living and growing plants, of sea grass. The plants are not often consumed until they die and fall to the seafloor, where bacteria and fungi break them down into simpler materials. Small animals eat these decomposers and benefit from the nutrients provided by the grasses. Most of the organisms that live in sea-grass beds are dependent on dead plant matter rather than living grasses as the basis of their food web.

Hard, rocky substrates support very different groups of living things than those that make their homes in soft bottom habitats. Most hard-bottom zones are rich in species that form attachments, like oysters, sponges, and corals. Several types of seaweed find good places to anchor themselves in rocky areas, and they in turn attract a variety of animals. Many of the seaweeds and sponges on hard substrates are encrusting forms that cover the surfaces of rocks like films or crusts.

Kelp, a tall, brown seaweed, thrives on rocky substrates because it is able to establish a firm hold on the substrate. Because kelp is an extremely fast-growing plant, it needs a lot of nutrients. That is why kelp habitats are often found in areas where nutrients upwell. Kelp takes in nutrients by simply absorbing them directly from the water. The number and diversity of living things found among kelp beds is enormous and forms communities that include familiar organisms like crabs, sea stars, turtles, sponges, snails, and octopuses.

Coral reefs are structures made from the skeletons of millions of dead coral organisms. Each coral animal, which is

Biodiversity

Biodiversity, or biological diversity, refers to the variety of living things in an area. Diversity is higher in complex environments than in simple ones. Complex physical environments have a lot to offer organisms in the way of food and housing. Estuaries, shorelines, and coral reefs are extremely complex marine environments, and each of them provides a wide assortment of nutritional resources for living things.

There are thousands of habitats in estuaries, coastal systems where fresh and salt water meet and mix. The bottom of the estuary provides homes for different kinds of organisms. Some spend their entire lives on the surface of the sediment, many burrow just under the surface, and others dig deep into the sediment. Organisms also select locations that accommodate their abilities to tolerate salt, so those that are adapted to high salinity are on the seaward side while the freshwater-dependent ones are on the river side. In between the two extremes, organisms live in zones that meet the salinity requirements for their bodies.

Diversity is an important aspect of a healthy ecosystem. In an ecosystem where all living things are exactly the same, one big change in the environment could cause widespread destruction. This might be best understood in a familiar ecosystem, like a forest. If only one kind of tree is growing in the forest, a virus that damages that type of plant could wipe out the entire forest. If the forest contains 20 different kinds of trees, it is unlikely that one disease agent could destroy the entire plant community. A high degree of biodiversity gives an ecosystem an edge, ensuring that it can continue to exist and function regardless of changes around it.

about the same size as an ant, secretes a calcium carbonate skeleton around its body for protection. As one generation of coral animals dies, the next generation continues building the reef by adding a new layer to the existing ones. Because reefs offer a tremendous number of habitats, they are environments that support high species diversity.

Conclusion

Although the waters over continental margins make up only a small portion of the seas, they are homes to diverse and large populations of organisms. Neritic waters are extremely productive areas that are rich in nutrients provided by the land and the ocean. Almost all the species found in other marine environments, whether they be open sea or coastal, can also be located in the waters of continental margins at some point in their lives.

The continental margin environment is characterized by several important chemical and physical properties. Salinity, the amount of dissolved minerals in water, can vary slightly because of the proximity to the coast. Freshwater entering neritic zones can reduce the salinity, but periods of low rainfall or seasons of high evaporative rates can increase it. The temperatures of neritic waters are warmer than those of the open ocean, but not as warm as shallow coastal or estuary water. Temperatures vary somewhat with geographic location and season.

Neritic waters are usually brown or green in color because they contain large populations of organisms and sediment. Suspended matter in the water affects the amount of light that can penetrate it. Sediment in the water primarily comes from erosion of soil on the land. Simple, green microscopic organisms thrive in neritic waters because these are the places where supplies of nutrients are abundant. The green microscopic organisms provide food that supports animal-like microorganisms.

Because the waters are relatively shallow and nutrient loads from land are high, neritic waters are very productive. Several kinds of plants, including sea grasses, kelps, and other seaweeds, grow there. Despite this abundance of plant material, few large grazers feed on the plants. Instead, most plant matter dies and falls to the bottom, where it provides food for decomposers.

The communities of organisms that develop in continental margin waters depend to a degree on the kinds of substrates found there. Open, sedimentary environments may be largely unvegetated, supporting only green one-celled inhabitants. In such locations, there are more animals living in or under the soil than on top of it.

Some soft substrates support lush underwater meadows of grass. Sea grasses have a significant environmental impact on an area because they slow the movement of water and increase the deposition of sediments. Sea grasses also provide good hiding places for many young fish and shellfish. Hard, rocky substrates support populations of animals that need to attach to the seabed. Rocky substrates may be the sites of kelp beds, thick forests of tall, brown seaweed. Kelp forests provide homes for rich communities of life forms that include shellfish, fish, and marine mammals.

One of the most colorful and diverse neritic environments is the coral reef. Made from the skeletons of millions of tiny animals, coral reefs provide habitats for a variety of other kinds of organisms that feed on the coral, prey on the coral animals, or graze on the associated sponges.

All the marine regions found within the continental shelves are highly populated. Most of the living things depend on energy from the Sun to support a variety of green organisms. The types, and characteristics, of these organisms are dependent on the amount of sunlight and nutrients found in the water as well as its temperature and salinity.

2

Microbes and Plants
The Beginning and End of Continental Shelf Food Chains

$\mathcal{T}$ he continental shelves are recipients of nutrients and minerals from both the landmasses they border and from the open sea. These life-sustaining provisions support dense populations of one-celled organisms that are capable of making their own food. The countless green cells that float in the enriched waters, along with the organisms that graze on them, make up the plankton. Plankton forms the base of a food web that supports thousands of other types of organisms.

The term *plankton,* derived from the Greek for "wanderer" or "drifter," refers to the free-floating lifestyle of the inhabitants. Members of the plankton lack a point of attachment, so they never settle in one place. They also lack a method of propelling themselves through the water. Even though many species of plankton can travel up and down in the water column, their horizontal positions are determined by action of the water.

The plankton community is subdivided into zooplankton, the animal-like organisms, and phytoplankton, those that contain chlorophyll. Both groups are made up of unicellular and small, multicellular organisms. Most spend the majority of their time floating in the upper levels of the water column, where phytoplankton can get as much sunlight as possible.

Phytoplankton are responsible for much of the *productivity* of the marine environment as a whole. As a group, they carry out 40 percent of the photosynthesis in the sea. Composed of more than 5,000 different species, the total mass of phytoplankton exceeds that of all the marine animals combined, including fish and mammals. Figure 2.1 shows some typical forms of plankton.

Some of the dominant species of phytoplankton include the dinoflagellates and diatoms. Dinoflagellates are more common in warm water than diatoms, which favor cool regions.

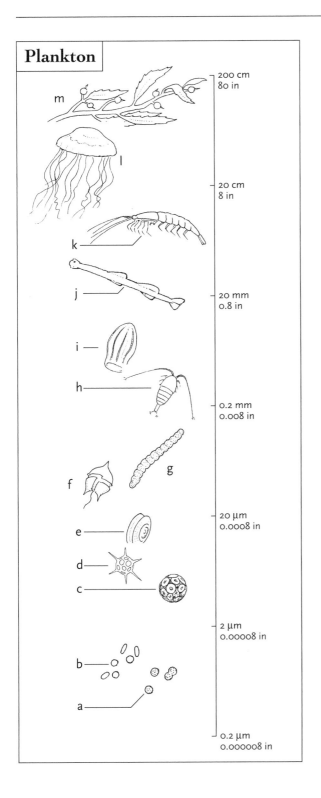

Plankton

m

l

k

j

i

h

g

f

e

d

c

b

a

200 cm
80 in

20 cm
8 in

20 mm
0.8 in

0.2 mm
0.008 in

20 μm
0.0008 in

2 μm
0.00008 in

0.2 μm
0.000008 in

Cyanobacteria, green cells that are smaller than either diatoms or dinoflagellates, also make up a large percentage of the phytoplankton worldwide.

Simple Producers

Bacteria, the most numerous organisms on Earth, flourish in the waters of the continental shelves. As the simplest forms of life, bacteria are also the smallest organisms. Because their cells lack membrane-bound structures, DNA of bacteria is not contained within nuclei. All the photosynthesizing species, a group collectively known as *cyanobacteria*, contain chlorophyll that floats freely in the cells. The presence of chlorophyll means that the cells can produce food for themselves as well as supply food to other kinds of organisms that graze on them.

Fig. 2.1   *Plankton includes all of the organisms that float in the surface waters. The smallest organisms are the bacteria (a) and cyanobacteria (b). Significantly larger are the one-celled coccolithophores (c), flagellates (d), diatoms (e), dinoflagellates (f), and colonial cyanobacteria (g). Copepods (h), comb jellies (i), and arrow worms (j) are some of the smallest animals that can be seen with the naked eye. Krill (k), large jellyfish (l), and floating seaweed (m) are much more obvious.*

Food Chains and Photosynthesis

Living things must have energy to survive. In an ecosystem, the path that energy takes as it moves from one organism to another is called a food chain. The Sun is the major source of energy for most food chains. Organisms that can capture the Sun's energy are called producers, or autotrophs, because they are able to produce food molecules. Living things that cannot capture energy must eat food and are referred to as consumers, or heterotrophs. Heterotrophs that eat plants are herbivores, and those that eat animals are carnivores. Organisms that eat plants and animals are described as omnivores.

When living things die, another group of organisms in the food chain—the decomposers, or detritivores—uses the energy tied up in the lifeless bodies. Detritivores break down dead or decaying matter, returning the nutrients to the environment. Nutrients in ecosystems are constantly recycled through interlocking food chains called food webs. Energy, on the other hand, cannot be recycled. It is eventually lost to the system in the form of heat.

Autotrophs can capture the Sun's energy because they contain the green pigment chlorophyll. During photosynthesis, detailed in Figure 2.2, autotrophs use the Sun's energy to rearrange the carbon atoms from carbon dioxide gas to form glucose molecules. Glucose is the primary food or energy source for living things. The hydrogen and oxygen atoms needed to form glucose come from molecules of water. Producers give off the extra oxygen atoms that are generated during photosynthesis as oxygen gas.

Autotrophs usually make more glucose than they need, so they store some for later use. Heterotrophs consume this stored glucose to support their own life processes. In the long run, it is an ecosystem's productivity that determines the types and numbers of organisms that can live there.

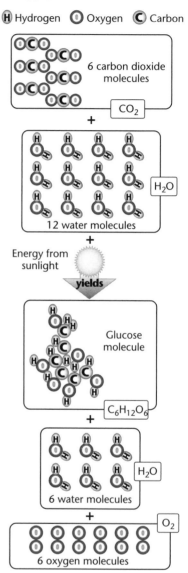

Fig. 2.2   *During photosynthesis, the energy of sunlight is used to rearrange the components of carbon dioxide and water molecules to form glucose, water, and oxygen.*

Growing singly or in colonies, cyanobacteria are the most abundant members of the phytoplankton. Each cell of cyanobacteria contains chlorophyll as well as accessory pigments that enhance their ability to capture light. The accessory pigments are responsible for the variety of colors found in cyanobacteria, including shades of brown, gold, black, and blue-green.

A few species of cyanobacteria perform another valuable function in the neritic zones: They capture nitrogen gas and make it available to other living things. Because nitrogen is essential for growth and development, lack of the element often limits the number of organisms living in an environment. Nitrogen gas is abundant in both the atmosphere and in ocean water, but living things cannot utilize nitrogen in the gaseous form. Nitrogen-fixing bacteria in the environment can convert gaseous nitrogen into a form that other living things can use. In a sense, these organisms act as fertilizers, enriching the waters with nitrogen and promoting the growth of producers. The cells that perform this task are related to species of bacteria that carry out the same function in the roots of legumes, like beans.

One type of nitrogen-fixing cyanobacteria is called "sea sawdust" (*Trichodesmium*). So named because their colonies resemble sawdust floating on the water's surface, these cyanobacteria provide nitrogen in tropical and subtropical waters, where supplies of the element are generally low. *Lyngbya majuscule* is a bottom-dwelling species of nitrogen-fixing cyanobacteria. Individual cells of *Lyngbya* are enclosed in unbranched, mucus-covered filaments. Olive-colored strands of *Lyngbya* can form mats on the shelf floors, especially in shallow regions.

Chemosynthesizers

Most producers are photosynthesizers, green organisms that rely on the Sun as their source of energy. A much smaller group of organisms are classified as chemosynthesizers because they get the energy to make food from chemical compounds instead of from sunlight. Since these cells do not require the Sun's energy, they can operate in dark environments, like those found within sediments. Many chemosynthesizers are also capable of carrying out their life processes in the absence of oxygen.

One such group, the sulfur bacteria, are able to gather energy by converting sulfate compounds into sulfide compounds. Because sulfate compounds constantly erode into the waters of the continental shelves from land, the activities of sulfur bacteria help keep levels in check. Sulfur bacteria also have key roles in food webs because they serve as sources of food for many zooplankton.

Beggiatoa species are sulfur bacteria that form large colonies on top of sulfur-rich sediments. Found at several depths over the continental shelves, *Beggiatoa* are relatively large in the world of bacteria. Depending on the species, they

Kingdoms of Living Things

There are millions of different kinds of living things on Earth. To study them, scientists called taxonomists classify organisms by their characteristics. The first taxonomist was Carolus Linnaeus (1707–78), a Swedish naturalist who separated all creatures into two extremely large groups, or kingdoms: Plantae (plants) and Animalia (animals). By the middle of the 19th century, these two kingdoms had been joined by the newly designated Protista, the microscopic organisms, and Fungi. When microscopes advanced to the point that taxonomists could differentiate the characteristics of microorganisms, Protista was divided to include the kingdom Monera. By 1969, a five-kingdom classification system made up of Monera (bacteria), Protista (protozoans), Fungi, Animalia, and Plantae was established. The five-kingdom system is still in use today, although most scientists prefer to separate monerans into two groups, the kingdom Archaebacteria and the kingdom Eubacteria.

Monerans are the smallest creatures on Earth, and their cells are much simpler than the cells of other living things. Monerans that cannot make their own food are known as bacteria and include organisms such as *Escherichia coli* and *Bacillus anthracis.* Photosynthetic monerans are collectively called cyanobacteria, and include *Anabaena affinis* and *Leptolyngbya fragilis.* In the six-kingdom classification system, the most common monerans, those that live in water, soil, and on other living things, are placed in the kingdom Eubacteria. Archaebacteria are the inhabitants of may form clumps or filaments, many of which appear whitish in color because light is reflected off the sulfur compounds within them.

Symbiotic Monerans

A few species of monerans are symbiotic with marine plants and animals. *Symbiosis* is a close relationship between two organisms of different species. In most cases of cyanobacterial symbiosis, relationships are mutually beneficial arrangements that provide the bacterial cells with protection and housing and the host cells with food.

Cyanobacteria that live as symbionts can be found in a few species of protists, as well as in the tissues of some worms, sponges, and other animals. Sponges of many varieties team

extreme situations, such as hot underwater geothermal vents or extremely salty lakebeds.

Another kingdom of one-celled organisms, Protista, includes amoeba, euglena, and diatoms. Unlike monerans, protists are large, complex cells that are structurally like the cells of multicellular organisms. Members of the Protista kingdom are a diverse group varying in mobility, size, shape, and feeding strategies. A number are autotrophs, some heterotrophs, and others are mixotrophs, organisms that can make their own food and eat other organisms, depending on the conditions dictated by their environment.

The Fungi kingdom consists primarily of multicelled organisms, like molds and mildews, but there are a few one-celled members, such as the yeasts. Fungi cannot move around, and they are unable to make their own food because they do not contain chlorophyll. They are heterotrophs that feed by secreting digestive enzymes on organic material, then absorbing that material into their bodies.

The other two kingdoms, Plantae and Animalia, are also composed of multicelled organisms. Plants, including seaweeds, trees, and dandelions, do not move around but get their food by converting the Sun's energy into simple carbon compounds. Therefore, plants are autotrophs. Animals, on the other hand, cannot make their own food. These organisms are heterotrophs, and they include fish, whales, and humans, all of which must actively seek the food they eat.

Bioluminescence

A few organisms have the ability to bioluminesce, or produce their own light. In the marine environment, light-producers include bacteria, phytoplankton, invertebrates, and fish. Bioluminescent light results from a chemical reaction that occurs within cells. A protein, luciferin, reacts with an enzyme, luciferase, in the presence of oxygen. A molecule of luciferin can only be used one time, and in most organisms new luciferin must be provided for each reaction. In some cases, luciferin and luciferase are chemically bound to one another as a large molecule called a photoprotein. Calcium and some other ions are able to trigger photoproteins to react. Most of the energy of the reaction is released as light, with very little wasted in the form of heat.

Scientists hypothesize that light-generating reactions must be important to the survival of organisms that use them because the very act of making light consumes up to 10 percent of their energy. No one knows for certain the purpose of light production, but four theories have been suggested. Light may help organisms evade their predators, attract their prey, communicate with others of their own species, or advertise. An anglerfish, which lives in deep water, where little or no light penetrates, attracts prey by dangling a glowing, lurelike appendage near its mouth. When an unsuspecting fish comes by to inspect it, the anglerfish lunges forward and engulfs it.

Flashlight fish have patches under their eyes that are filled with light-producing bacteria. The fish can control the amount of light emitted from the patches by raising or lowering lids that can cover them. These animals may use blinking signals as a form of communication, similar to the flashes produced by fireflies. A dinoflagellate, *Noctiluca,* glows when a wave or boat jostles the water, or when a fish swims nearby. The light it releases may help confuse predators swimming in its midst.

The amount of light produced by bioluminescence is significant. Even though the glow from a single dinoflagellate lasts only 0.1 seconds, it is visible to the human eye. Larger organisms, like jellyfish, emit greater quantities of light. Jellyfish and other large organisms may glow for tens of seconds.

Most of the light produced by living things is blue. Underwater blue light can travel farther than any other color, so light produced in shades of blue is carried the greatest possible distance. In addition, most marine organisms are adapted to see shades of blue but are blind to other colors. An exception to this rule is a fish known as loosejaw that gives off, and is capable of seeing, red light. Humans cannot see the glow of loosejaws because the shade of red it emits is close to the infrared portion of the electromagnetic spectrum. This fish may be better camouflaged than any other bioluminescent organism since it produces a light that helps it see its own species and possibly its prey, while it cannot be seen by other organisms.

up with several types of cyanobacteria, including those of the genera *Aphanocapsa, Synechocystis, Oscillatoria,* and *Phormidium.* All these cyanobacteria, except for *Phormidium,* live alongside the cells of their hosts. As the cyanobacterial cells carry out photosynthesis, much of the food they produce leaks out and is absorbed by the sponge cells. In the case of *Phormidium,* the relationship between cyanobacteria and host is even closer. Members of this species live in tiny, membrane-bound sacks located inside the cells of their host sponges.

Food is just one benefit that bacteria have to offer their hosts. Some monerans are bioluminescent, or able to produce light. Bioluminescent bacteria live in the bodies of several kinds of organisms, including bony fish, sharks, and protists.

Simple Consumers

Not all kinds of the bacteria are producers like cyanobacteria or the chemosynthesizing species. Some types of bacteria must ingest their food. Heterotrophic bacteria fill their nutritional needs by feeding on a variety of materials, including dead or decaying plants and animals, other bacteria, and dissolved nutrients. As a group, heterotrophic bacteria are vitally important to the process of decomposition. By breaking down complex compounds, they release inorganic nutrients such as phosphorous and nitrogen, enabling these materials to be recycled in the environment. In addition, heterotrophic bacteria serve as a source of food for organisms like protozoans and small shellfish.

Protists and Fungi

Hundreds of species of large cells called protists live among the bacteria in the plankton and on the seafloor. Many, such as diatoms and dinoflagellates are producers, responsible for much of the photosynthesis in the neritic waters. Others, including foraminiferans, coccolithophores, and radiolarians, are consumers.

Most commonly found in cool marine waters, diatoms possess chlorophyll as well as a yellow-brown pigment that is responsible for their golden color. Although there are literally thousands of species of diatoms, all share some common traits. Diatoms are unicellular organisms that build silica shells, called frustules, around themselves. Some diatoms are round and their two-part frustules resemble the lids and bases of glass pill boxes. Others, like *Chaetocerus lorenzianus,* are long, narrow diatoms whose shape is described as pinnate.

Diatoms serve as food for a number of organisms, including members of the zooplankton. Consumers rarely have trouble locating diatoms because they float in the upper part of the water column in full sunlight. To provide the *buoyancy* needed to float, each diatom cell produces a small amount of oil. Many diatoms possess ornate whorls and extensions from their frustules, structures that help prevent the cells from sinking. Diatoms that are not consumed by predators eventually die, and their shells fall to the seafloor. Mud and sediment that contains accumulated diatoms shells is called diatomaceous earth, and it is mined as a material that is used to make filters and abrasives.

In warm, tropical waters, dinoflagellates are more common than diatoms. Possessing pigments that give them colors varying from red to green, dinoflagellates are important primary producers in tropical and temperate waters. Some species of dinoflagellates are not completely dependent on photosynthesis for their food. These organisms can absorb nutrients from the water or capture small food items to help meet their nutritional needs.

Dinoflagellates can be found floating in the upper water column. Most have a smooth, flexible armor made of cellulose, a compound that is also found in plants, and two *flagella* for mobility. Long, bristlelike extensions from their armor serve two purposes; they help prevent the cells from sinking and they discourage predators.

When environmental conditions are just right, several kinds of algae and protists, including dinoflagellates, reproduce rapidly, creating a dense population called an *algal bloom*. The mass of microbes in seawater affects the water's color. Shades of red are common among dinoflagellates and have led to the general designation of "red tide" for any bloom. Scientists prefer to call such events harmful algal blooms (HABs) because tides are not involved in the phenomena and colors can vary from green to brown, depending on the species of organisms involved.

Algal blooms may be harmful for two reasons. Autotrophs like dinoflagellates produce oxygen during the day as a by-product of photosynthesis, but at night oxygen production stops. In the process of respiration, algal cells consume oxygen both day and night. When populations of cells are extremely large, oxygen supplies in the water can be depleted at night, causing the death of the algae as well as other oxygen-dependent organisms like fish and shellfish.

Another way that HABs can damage organisms is by releasing toxins. Only a few of the more than 1,000 species of dinoflagellates are capable of producing toxins. The chemicals these dinoflagellates produce have no effect on shellfish like clams and oysters that feed on the cells, but can be dangerous to fish, birds, marine mammals, and humans that consume the shellfish. Some of the conditions caused by blooms of dinoflagellates include paralytic shellfish poisoning, amnesic shellfish poisoning, ciguatera fish poisoning, diarrheic shellfish poisoning, and neurotoxic shellfish poisoning. Figure 2.3 details the events of a HAB.

In many cases, algal blooms include large populations of relatively harmless dinoflagellates such as *Noctiluca scintillans,* a bioluminescent species. Experiments show that the protists do not emit light during the day when it could not be seen, leading many researchers to believe that the light has an important job. The light may simply be a method of confusing predators, but some scientists have suggested an alternate view. Their police and burglar theory suggests that the cells produce light when small, plankton-eating predators (the burglars) are close by. The light attracts the attention of larger predators (the police) that can feed on, and eliminate, the organisms that are direct threats to the protists.

Fig. 2.3   Some dinoflagellate species produce red tides. (a) During red tides, the numbers of dinoflagellates increase dramatically (1). When red tides subside, their constituent phytoplankton die off (2) and serve as food for bacteria. Large populations of bacteria can quickly use up all the oxygen in the water, killing fish and shellfish (3). (b) Some dinoflagellates contain toxins that attack the nervous systems of vertebrates, but not most invertebrates. Shellfish can consume the toxic dinoflagellates without being harmed (1). When vertebrates, including fish, birds, marine mammals, and humans, consume the shellfish, they are poisoned (2).

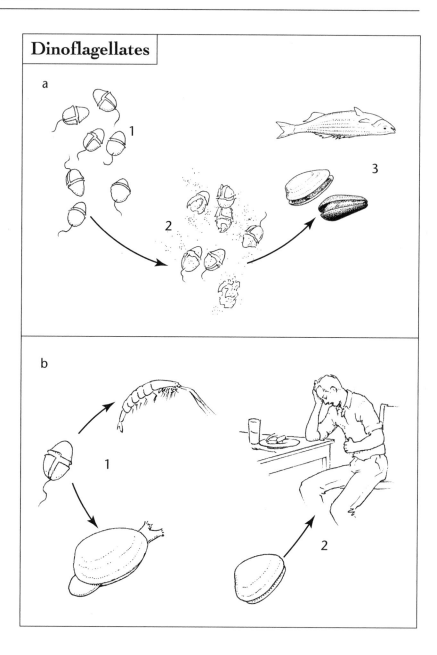

Dinoflagellates

Numerous species of dinoflagellates live in symbiotic relationships within the tissues of other organisms. Corals, anemones, sponges, and other animals support *zooxanthellae,* a variety of one-celled organisms that produce food for themselves as well as their hosts. Dinoflagellates that live as zooxanthellae lose their armor and flagella and exist in the "naked" state. Many animals that host dinoflagellates are completely dependent on these tiny producers to support their nutritional needs and cannot survive without them. On the other hand, the protists are capable of leaving their hosts, and sometimes do so. If this happens, the cells regain their armor and flagella and return to independent life in the water column.

Like most species of protists, dinoflagellates undergo *asexual reproduction* by *binary fission*. In the armored species, each daughter cell gets half the armor, then makes the other half of the shell. *Sexual reproduction* occurs if two cells fuse to form a single large cell that contains the DNA of both parental cells. The large cell splits into two daughter cells, each with new combinations of DNA.

Another group of photosynthetic protists are the coccolithophores, organisms covered with microscopic calcium carbonate plates. Each plate or coccolith is shaped like a tiny hubcap that is only three one-thousandths of a millimeter wide. Like many other types of phytoplankton, dense populations of coccolithophores live at the surface of the water.

One species, *Emiliania huxley,* or Ehux, flourishes best in nutrient-poor waters of mild and subpolar climate zones, although it can be found in shelf waters worldwide. During blooms, dense masses of Ehux cells may cover sections of the ocean as large as 100,000 square miles (258,998.8 km²), an area the size of England. Blooms are easy to recognize, especially during the day, when the white calcium carbonate plates change the color of water to milky turquoise. At night, the white shells twinkle as they reflect moonlight. Each Ehux cell like other coccolithophores, makes a coccolith inside a specialized sac. When a coccolith is complete, the sac fuses with the cell membrane, then extrudes the platelet to the exterior. During times of plenty when nutrient levels are extremely high, cells produce more platelets than they need. The extra pieces remain loosely attached to the armor until they are shaken loose by waves. Extra shells, along with the shells of dead cells, accumulate in thick layers on the seafloor.

Other kinds of protists that live in the continental waters include amoeba-like organisms such as foraminifera and radiolarians. Unlike diatoms, dinoflagellates, and coccolithophores, forams and radiolarians do not contain chlorophyll. For this reason, they are consumers and make up part of the zooplankton. Both types of organisms feed by absorbing nutrients from the water and by engulfing tiny bits of food.

Foraminifera (forams) are cells that live in shells, or tests, made of calcium carbonate. The tests of forams vary tremendously from one species to the next, some small, one-chambered structures, while others are multichambered. Several species of forams secrete their shells but some construct them by gluing together sand and other particles. Foram shells can reach a half-inch in length, so are visible with the naked eye, an unusual property for protists.

Depending on the species, continental shelf foraminifera float in the water, grow on rocks, colonize the surfaces of seaweeds, or live in the sediment. They move by sending out pseudopods, extensions of their cytoplasm, through tiny holes in their shells. Pseudopods enable forams to inch their way along substrates. When the cells of forams die, their shells settle to the seafloor to form layers that may cover thousands of square miles. The white cliffs of Dover were formed from soil made up of fossils of accumulated foram shells. Because the size and structure of foram tests vary with water temperatures, scientists often use fossilized shells to determine the temperatures of ocean waters in the past.

Radiolarians are also amoeboid protists, but their tests are made of silica. To deter predators and slow their rate of sinking, the tests of radiolarians are studded with tiny spines and other projections. The tests are perforated with holes through which the organisms extend pseudopods to capture food.

Not all protists are protected by shells or tests. Ciliates are protists that are covered in short, hairlike structures called *cilia*. The beating motion of cilia provides these cells with weak locomotion and also sweeps food particles toward the mouthlike oral groove. Ciliates can be found in many different parts of the environment, including the water column, the substrate, and attached to the gills of several kinds of animals. As predators, they usually feed on monerans. By doing so, ciliates help make the nutrition contained in the extremely small moneran cells available to members of the food chain that are unable to feed directly on such tiny prey.

One ciliate, *Strombidium capitatum,* is a heterotroph that has an unusual nutritional strategy. Instead of digesting the chloroplasts of its prey, *Strombidium* leaves them intact and uses the structures in its own body to produce food. In this way, the ciliate creates a backup plan for times when food supplies are limited.

Fungi, which can be single or multicellular organisms, include the familiar terrestrial molds and mildews. There are about 500 species of fungi in the marine environment, most of which function in roles very similar to those of bacterial decomposers. Like bacteria, fungi are important mediators of energy flow through the marine ecosystems. As they break down organic matter and change it into simpler materials for their own use, they also release nutrients and minerals into the environment. Many organisms get their energy by feeding on fungi. A few species of marine fungi are parasitic on sea plants, fish, sponges, and shellfish.

Like all fungi, marine fungi extend thin filaments called *hyphae.* Each fungal filament releases enzymes that dissolve material, liquefying it to be absorbed by fungal cells. Fungi can reproduce sexually or asexually. When cells of two different mating types meet, they form a mating bridge between them. The nucleus of one cell crosses the bridge to fuse with the nucleus of the other cell. Fruiting bodies that develop from this cell produce spores that generate new fungi. In some cases, spores are also produced by structures that arise from asexual cells of fungi. In marine fungi, spores show special adaptations, such as appendages, that either help them float or enable them to cling to substrates.

Plants

Although phytoplankton are important producers on the continental shelves, they are not the only ones. Several species of marine plants flourish in the nutrient-rich waters. In the relatively shallow waters of the continental shelf, plants have access to plenty of sunlight. In addition, many can find firm points of attachment, giving them a base from which to grow.

Differences in Terrestrial and Aquatic Plants

Even though plants that live in water look dramatically different from terrestrial plants, the two groups have a lot in common. Both types of plants capture the Sun's energy and use it to make food from raw materials. In each case, the raw materials required include carbon dioxide, water, and minerals. The differences in these two types of plants are adaptations to their specific environments.

Land plants are highly specialized for their lifestyles. They get their nutrients from two sources: soil and air. It is the job of roots to absorb water and minerals from the soil, as well as hold the plant in place. Essential materials are transported to cells in leaves by a system of tubes called vascular tissue. Leaves are in charge of taking in carbon dioxide gas from the atmosphere for photosynthesis. Once photosynthesis is complete, a second set of vascular tissue carries the food made by the leaves to the rest of the plant. Land plants are also equipped with woody stems and branches that hold them upright so that they can receive plenty of light.

Marine plants, called macroalgae or seaweeds, get their nutrients, water, and dissolved gases from seawater. Since water surrounds the entire marine plant, these dissolved nutrients simply diffuse into each cell. For this reason, marine plants do not have vascular tissue to accommodate

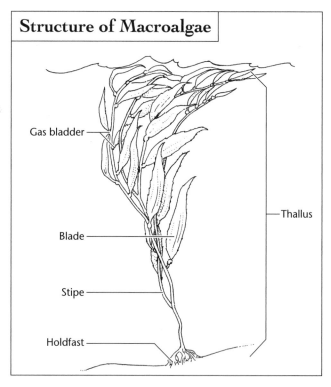

Structure of Macroalgae

Gas bladder

Thallus

Blade

Stipe

Holdfast

Fig. 2.4   *The body, or thallus, of a macroalga is made up of leaflike blades, stemlike stipes, and rootlike holdfasts. Gas bladders on the stipes and blades help hold the plant near the top of the water column.*

photosynthesis or to carry its products to each cell. In addition, marine plants do not need support structures because they are held up by the buoyant force of the water. Since water in the ocean is always moving, the bodies of marine plants are flexible, permitting them to go with that movement. Some marine plants secrete mucus to make their surfaces slick, further reducing their drag or resistance to water movement. Mucus also helps keep animals from eating them.

A plant that grows on land is described with terms such as *leaf, stem,* and *root.* Seaweeds are made up of different components, which are shown in Figure 2.4. The parts of seaweed that look like leaves are termed *blades,* or *fronds.* Some are equipped with small, gas-filled sacs, or *bladders,* that help keep them afloat and close to the sunlight. The gases in these bladders are usually nitrogen, argon, and oxygen. The stemlike structures of macroalgae are referred to as *stipes.* A root-shaped mass, the *holdfast,* anchors seaweeds but does not absorb nutrients like true roots do. Together, the blades, stipes, and holdfast make up the body, or *thallus,* of the macroalgae. Thalli take on many different forms, including tall and branched or thin and flat.

Marine plants fall into two major types: macroscopic algae and vascular plants. Macroscopic algae, or seaweeds, are multicellular autotrophs with unique adaptations for their marine habitats. Seaweeds are classified as green, red, and brown, depending on the pigments they contain. Vascular plants, another group of multicellular autotrophs, include several types of sea grasses.

Green Algae

Green algae are closely related to terrestrial plants because they share the same major pigments, chlorophyll a, chlorophyll b, and carotenoids. Although many species of green algae are unicellular and difficult to detect, green macroalgae are obvious and important producers on continental shelves. *Ulva,* or sea lettuce, is a macroalga that resembles bright green sheets of tissue paper with ruffled edges. Depending on the species, the plant may be from 11.8 inches (30 cm) to 39.4 inches (1 m) long. The extremely thin sheets of *Ulva* are made up of only two cell layers. A small, disc-shaped holdfast secures most types to the substrate, but free-floating species exist. Sea lettuce (*Ulva fenestrate*) and corkscrew sea lettuce (*Ulva taenjata*) are common on the continental shelf.

Dead man's fingers (various species of *Codium*) is a pale to dark green, bushlike macroalga that branches from a holdfast, forming plants up to 35.4 inches (90 cm) in height. Branches are cylindrical and fingerlike, with a soft, fuzzy texture. *Enteromorpha intestinalis,* which is characterized by bright green blades, produces tubular, unbranched fronds that resemble intestines. The fronds grow 3.9 to 11.8 inches (10 to 30 cm) long from small holdfasts that are secured to soil or rocks. Gases contained in the fronds help them float on the surface of the water.

Brown Algae

Kelp, sargassum weed, and rockweed, a few of the many types of brown algae, contain chlorophyll as well as accessory pigments that give them colors ranging from yellow to black. An extremely diverse group, some brown algae are tiny, microscopic organisms, while others reach lengths of 330 feet (100 m). Except for sargassum, most species prefer shallow, cool, or cold waters. Many types of brown algae produce chemicals for protection from predators.

Brown algae are well adapted for high-energy waters. The stipes and fronds synthesize a gellike material, alginate, that gives the plants flexibility so they can move with the flow of water. Alginate also conserves moisture, protecting the plants when the tide is out and conditions are dry. To maintain their height in the water column, fronds are equipped with air bladders.

For many people, the long, leathery kelp, featured in the upper color insert on page C-1, is the most familiar type of seaweed. Kelp, the largest alga in the world, forms important habitats on continental shelves where the water is cold, substrates are firm, and nutrients plentiful. Under these conditions, kelp can flourish, producing plants that are more than 330 feet (100 meters) long. Some kelp beds are so tall that they are described as "forests." Like terrestrial forests, kelp forests have upper-level canopies that shade the levels beneath them. The two largest types, giant kelp (*Macrocystis*) and bull kelp (*Nereocystis*), can grow at a rate of 19.5 inches (50 cm) a day. Along some North American coasts, kelps of the genus *Laminaria* dominate.

Kelp beds and forests are important sources of food in marine habitats. Only a few animals, such as sea urchins and some snails, are able to consume kelps. As the plants grow, the mature fronds fray at the edges, creating a steady stream of detritus into the food chain. This dead organic matter is a rich source of food for bacteria and supports complex food webs. Kelps also provide habitats for communities of sea otters, sea lions, whales, and kelp fish.

Sargassum or sargassum weed are common names for macroalgae in the genus *Sargassum,* which contains more than 500 species worldwide. Individual plants, with their yellow-brown leaves attached to dark brown stipes, may grow to be 19.7 feet (6 m) long. Plants grow from holdfasts attached to the bottom, but may break loose and float freely. Large clumps of sargassum, called rafts or "weed bands," accumulate where currents come together. In open water, the plants are held high in the water columns by berrylike gas bladders.

Sargassum mats form important habitats in the neritic seas, creating unique communities of organisms. These large brown algae provide protection and cover for animals living in open-water environments on the continental shelf. Many animals hide among the fronds, while others dine on the large populations of microbes that accumulate around them.

Red Algae

Even though they are most numerous in warm tropical waters, red algae can be found over continental shelves worldwide. The majority of the more than 4,000 species are less than 3.3 feet (1 m) in length. All are equipped with accessory light-catching pigments in various shades of red that enable the plants to absorb green and blue light. Reproductive strategies vary according to species, although most are complex and involve both gamete- and spore-producing phases. Many species manufacture compounds that are commercially harvested such as agar, which is used to form thick gels for growing microbes in laboratories, and carageenan, a thickening agent used in foods like ice cream and products such as lotions.

The red alga *Mastrocarpus* ranges in color from reddish brown to olive green. In this plant, the sporophyte and gametophyte stages are distinctly different. The sporophyte stage is crustlike, and looks somewhat like a coat of tar or dark paint flowing across a substrate. The gametophyte stage is a short, branched plant on which the male and female sections have different appearances. Female areas are covered in small, round bumps called papillae, while the male sections, which lack papillae, are often so thin that they fall apart when sperm are released into the water.

Sea Grasses

Another important producer on the continental shelf is a group of plants known as sea grasses, shown in the lower color insert on page C-1. These vascular plants are close descendants of land plants, so they have many typical terrestrial plant adaptations like roots and vascular systems. In addition, sea grasses form tiny, pollen-producing flowers that release their contents in the water. After pollination, fertilized eggs mature into seeds that float away from the parent plants, sink, and start new beds of grass.

Sea grasses shown in Figure 2.5, are well-adapted for marine life. They often form extensive, underwater meadows that resemble fields of grass or wheat. Horizontally growing underground stems called rhizomes anchor them securely to the substrate, enabling the grasses to flourish in areas of strong currents or energetic wave action. Leaves contain air chambers that hold them up in the water, increasing their exposure to sunlight. Teeming with life, sea grass beds create a mixture of habitats on the continental shelf, providing homes for unique communities of organisms. For this reason, they promote biodiversity on the continental shelf. In addition, the meadows provide shelter and food for the young of many fish and shellfish species. Roots of the plants also help keep sediments in place and reduce erosion. Leaves of sea grasses act as filters, slowing down water movement and causing sediments to drop out of the water column. The rich organic matter that is mixed with these sediments supplement the growth of the seaweeds and other organisms that settle there.

As primary producers on continental shelves, sea grasses provide food for two groups of organisms: grazers and detritivores. Manatees, dugongs, turtles, and a variety of fish feed directly on the plants themselves. When the leaves of the plants die, they fall to the bottom and become part of the detritus food web.

There are 58 species of sea grasses, many named either for animals that graze on them or their shapes. Common eelgrass (*Zostera marina*) is a large plant, with leaves reaching 3.2 feet (one m) in length. Narrow-leafed eelgrass (*Zostera angustifolia*) is smaller, usually only reaching one-third the size of common eelgrass. The oval leaves of manatee grass (*Syringodium filiforme*), which reach up to 20 inches (50 cm) in length, make it easy to distinguish from turtle grass (*Thalassia testudinum*), which has ribbonlike leaves that are slightly shorter. The leaves of paddle grass (*Halophilia decipiens*) are small and rounded, occurring in pairs.

Conclusion

Continental shelves, the edges of the landmasses, are relatively shallow seas rich in nutrients and capable of supporting phytoplankton, macroalgae, kelp, and sea grasses. Each type of producer serves as the base of food chains that provide for different kinds of continental shelf communities. Cyanobacteria and single-celled protists are some of the dominant organisms in phytoplankton. Cyanobacteria are the smallest and simplest autotrophs. Hundreds of species of cyanobacteria are found throughout neritic waters, including near the surface and on the seafloor.

Diatoms, dinoflagellates, and coccolithophores are single-celled protists in the phytoplankton. Diatoms, which secrete silica shells, are most common in cool waters. As water temperature increases, populations of dinoflagellates rise. Dinoflagellates can be found living in the water column, or as

Sea Grasses

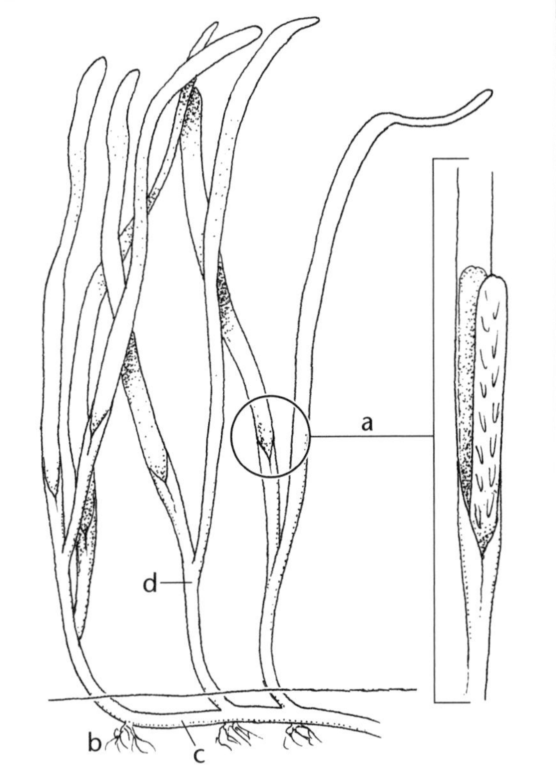

Fig. 2.5   Sea grasses are flowering plants that are descended from true land plants. Sea grasses produce flowers (a) that are pollinated underwater, have true roots (b) and underground branches called rhizomes (c), and give rise to new shoots (d).

symbionts in the tissues of several kinds of animals. Coccolithophores, which are covered with round calcium carbonate shells called coccoliths, favor mild and subtropical waters.

Heterotrophic bacteria and fungi play critically important roles as decomposers in continental shelf environments. As such, they release nutrients and minerals tied up in dead organisms, freeing them for reuse. Decomposers also serve as food for other types of small heterotrophs.

There are hundreds of types of seaweeds on the continental shelves, including species of green, red, and brown macroalgae. Kelp is a large, brown alga that forms forests where unique communities of organisms develop. Individual kelp plants are buoyed up in the water by gas bladders on their fronds that help keep them near the light. Sea grass is a vascular plant that is responsible for forming large undersea meadows. Like kelp forests, sea grass beds are critically important communities for large numbers of organisms. Sea grasses benefit the continental shelves by helping to hold soil in place and filtering the water.

3

Sponges, Cnidarians, and Worms
Simple and Successful Animals on the Continental Shelf

*B*ecause the continental shelf is a vast and varied space, it provides a countless array of habitats. Marine organisms arrange themselves in these habitats according to their needs and physical adaptations. The kinds of living things that flourish in sunny and shallow sublittoral waters have very different lifestyles from those that live in deeper waters, where less light infiltrates.

The largest group of animals on the continental shelf, as in the entire world, is the *invertebrates,* the animals without backbones. Globally, invertebrates outnumber vertebrates 10 to one. No one knows the exact number of invertebrates species, but estimates run from one to several million. Scientists point out that most marine invertebrates have probably not even been discovered yet.

Compared to vertebrates, the majority of invertebrates are small and inconspicuous. Many of the marine species are *sessile* organisms, nonmotile creatures that spend most of their lives in one place. Clams and scallops are some of the filter-feeding sessile invertebrates who strain the sea water for bits of organic matter. Anemones and corals are two of many predators that capture tiny fish or insectlike animals.

The marine invertebrates that are capable of locomotion, animals like crabs, shrimp, octopus, jellyfish, and worms, have a variety of nutritional strategies. Some are hunters that actively chase down their food, while others are wait-and-ambush–style predators that depend on camouflage and good hiding places to help them snare their next meal. Many active invertebrates feed on organic material that they find in the sediments, scooping up food-laden silt and sand with pincers, jaws, or tentacles. Others graze on phytoplankton or algae growing on undersea surfaces.

The roles of marine invertebrates are crucial in marine food chains. By consuming organic material, many of them help recycle the nutrients trapped in those materials. As they take suspended particles out of the sea water, filter-feeders help keep it clean. Invertebrates also act as prey for many larger animals in the food chain. Some types of organisms, such as corals, are responsible for building habitats where other organisms live.

The simplest invertebrates, sponges, cnidarians, and worms can be found in the water column as well as on the seafloor. Of the three groups, sponges are the most primitive. Sponges represent a transition between colonies of cells and animals with organized tissues. Cnidarians are more complex than sponges, equipped with mouths and simple digestive cavities. Worms are the most developed of the three types of organisms. They have definite head and tail ends, specialized body parts, and simple organ systems.

Sponges

Worldwide, there are about 15,000 species of sponges. Most live in soft sediments of the seafloor or attached to firm undersea substrates. At one time, sponges were mistaken for plants because they are immobile and many of them have plant-like shapes. Today the anatomy and physiology of these ancient animals are well understood.

The body of a sponge, shown in Figure 3.1, lacks tissues and organs, and functions in many ways like a colony of cells. The body wall is made up of an outer layer, the *epidermis,* an inner layer, the *gastrodermis,* and a jellylike layer between them called the *mesoglea.* The inner layer lines an interior cavity, while the outer layer is in contact with the environment.

Sponge body walls are supported by minute structures called *spicules* scattered throughout the mesoglea. Depending on the type of sponge, spicules can be made of calcium carbonate, silica, or a tough rubbery protein called spongin. The gastrodermis is lined with cells called *chaonocytes.* Chaonocytes are equipped with flagella, which they wave back and forth to keep water flowing through the animal, drawing it in through pores and sending it out through chimneylike openings called oscula.

Reproduction can occur sexually or asexually in sponges. Sexually, all sponges are *hermaphrodites,* producing both male and female sex cells. Depending on the species, either sperm, or both sperm and eggs, are released into the water. In both cases, the gametes find one another, fuse, and form zygotes. Zygotes develop into *larvae* that are *motile* and swim in the water column for a short time before settling to the bottom. Once they locate and attach to an appropriate substrate, sponges remain sessile for the rest of their lives.

A sponge can also reproduce asexually by forming buds, small organisms that grow at the base of the parent sponge. When buds are mature, they separate from the parent and live independently. In addition, sponges have tremendous powers of regeneration, so if a sponge is torn apart by waves, each part can develop into a new organism.

Because sponges are stationary, they are easy targets for hungry predators. Some species receive adequate protection from the sharp skeletal spicules that pierce their epidermis. Others produce chemicals that discourage animals from eating them. These toxins also keep plant spores or animal larvae from growing on the sponges and interfering with their development.

Sponges are scattered across the floor of the continental shelf at all depths where firm substrate is available. Their larvae will settle on any exposed surface, and they aggressively compete for space with other sessile organisms. Those in shallow, wave-tossed water tend to be low-growing, encrusting forms. In

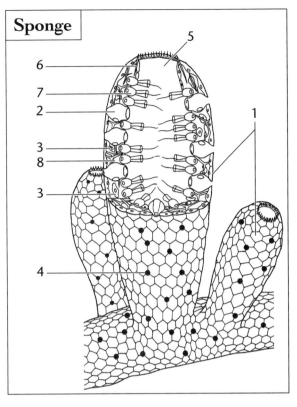

Sponge

Fig. 3.1   *The epidermis (1) of a sponge is filled with tiny pores called porocytes (2). Amoebocytes (3) move around the sponge carrying food to cells. Water enters the sponge through an incurrent pore (4), flows into the central cavity, and exits through the osculum (5). Spicules (6) lend support to the sponge's body wall. Choanocytes (7) lash their flagella in the central cavity to keep water moving through the sponge and to gather bits of food that are suspended in the water. The mesoglea (8) is a jellylike matrix located between the epidermis and the cells that line the central cavity.*

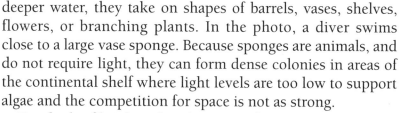

deeper water, they take on shapes of barrels, vases, shelves, flowers, or branching plants. In the photo, a diver swims close to a large vase sponge. Because sponges are animals, and do not require light, they can form dense colonies in areas of the continental shelf where light levels are too low to support algae and the competition for space is not as strong.

Hundreds of bright-colored species of sponges grow on and near coral reefs, lush communities of marine life that are situated on a few continental shelves in tropical waters. Coral reef communities are built around calcium carbonate structures created by the bodies and skeletons of coral animals. Some of the coral reef sponges include the tall, cylindrical giant tube sponge (*Aplysina lacunose*), which may be yellow, blue, or purple. The red strawberry sponge (*Mycales*) is covered with fleshy, thick-walled cylinders that look like tiny urns. The beautiful iridescent tube sponge (*Spinosella plicifera*) gives off a glow during the daylight. Boring sponges (*Cliona*) look like bright yellow patches growing on shellfish. This species bores into shells, weakening and often killing the occupants.

One type of sponge does not require a firm substrate, so it can be found in sand and silt sediments on some continental shelves. Sponges of the genus *Suberites* form associations with certain types of hermit crabs. Hermit crabs lack a protective shell over their abdomens, so they wear empty snail shells. *Suberites* sponges begin their lives by settling on snail shells and growing over their surfaces. Over

Fig. 3.2   A diver inspects a large vase sponge on the continental shelf. (Courtesy of OAR/National Undersea Research Program [NURP], NOAA)

time, sponges can completely engulf the shells and their original snail occupants. If the shells are taken by hermit crabs, the sponges remain in place, traveling with the crabs as they crawl along the seafloor. The sponges benefit from this relationship because they have the opportunity to move about, increasing their chances of finding food. The crabs benefit from the camouflage and the protection from predators provided by the sponges.

Because they lack nerves and other tissues, scientists have always considered sponges to be relatively insensitive to what is happening in their environment. Recent studies by Sally Leys and George O. Mackie of the University of Alberta have shown that one glass sponge, *Rhabdocalyptus dawsoni*, a resident of the continental shelf off the coast of Vancouver Island, responds to danger by generating electrical signals. Glass or hexactinosan sponges are distinguished from other types by their silica, or glasslike, spicules. Experiments show that when *Rhabdocalyptus dawsoni* is touched, its flagella stop moving. This response is probably a protective one that prevents

Fig. 3.3　The world's oceans are subdivided into five basins: the Pacific Ocean (1), the Atlantic Ocean (2), the Indian Ocean (3), the Arctic Ocean (4), and the Southern Ocean (5), which is made up of the most southerly reaches of the Pacific, Atlantic, and Indian Oceans.

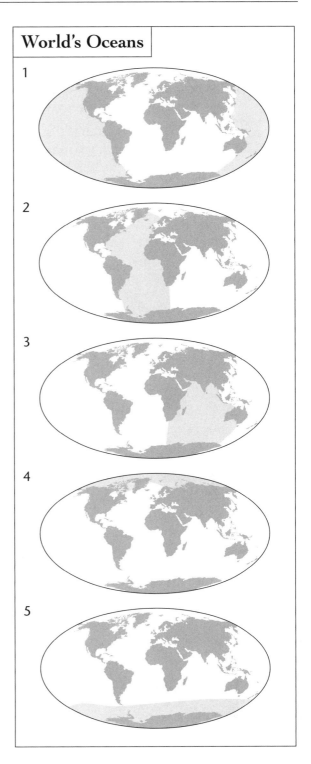

World's Oceans

Body Symmetry

An important characteristic of the body plan of an animal is its symmetry. Symmetry refers to the equivalence in size and shape of sections of an animal's body. Most animals exhibit body symmetry, but a few species of sponges are asymmetrical. If a plane were passed through the body of an asymmetrical sponge, slicing it in two, the parts would not be the same.

Some animals are radially symmetrical. Shaped like either short or long cylinders, these stationary or slow-moving organisms have distinct top and bottom surfaces but lack fronts and backs, heads or tails. A plane could pass through a radially symmetrical animal in several places to create two identical halves. Starfish, jellyfish, sea cucumbers, sea lilies, and sand dollars are a few examples of radially symmetrical animals.

The bodies of most animals are bilaterally symmetrical, a form in which a plane could pass through the animal only in one place to divide it into two equal parts. The two halves of a bilaterally symmetrical animal are mirror images of each other. Bilateral symmetry is associated with animals that move around. The leading part of a bilaterally symmetrical animal's body contains sense organs such as eyes and nose. Fish, whales, birds, snakes, and humans are all bilaterally symmetrical.

Scientists have special terms to describe the body of a bilaterally symmetrical animal, depicted in Figure 3.4. The head or front region is called the anterior portion and the opposite end, the hind region, is the posterior. The stomach or underside is the ventral side, and opposite that is the back, or dorsal, side. Structures located on the side of an animal are described as lateral.

Fig. 3.4 A sponge (a) is an asymmetrical animal. Starfish and jellyfish (b) are radially symmetrical; snails, turtles, and fish (c) are bilaterally symmetrical. In a bilaterally symmetrical animal, the head or front end is described as anterior and the tail end as posterior. The front or stomach side is ventral and the back or top side is dorsal. The sides of the animal are described as lateral.

Symmetries of Animals

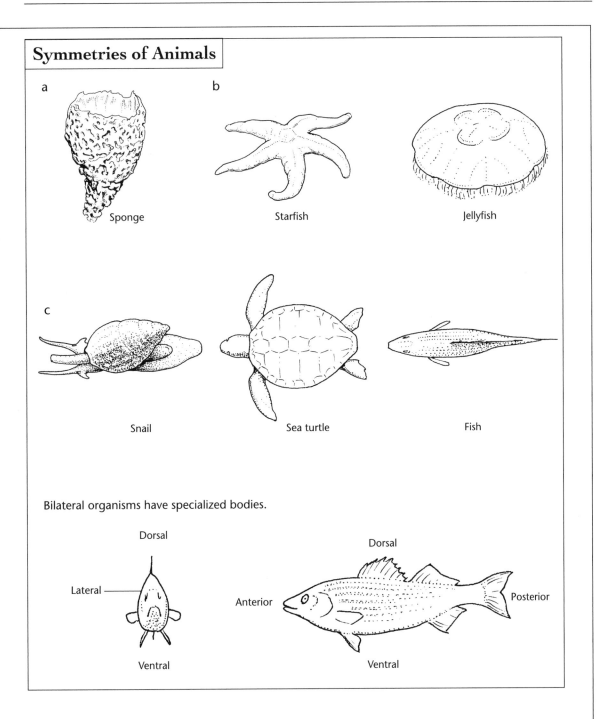

a

Sponge

b

Starfish

Jellyfish

c

Snail

Sea turtle

Fish

Bilateral organisms have specialized bodies.

Dorsal

Lateral

Ventral

Dorsal

Anterior

Posterior

Ventral

the sponge from pulling in sandy or silty water through its pores, clogging them. The presence of a probing predator could disturb and cloud the water. The signal to stop flagella movement is sent out through a network of fine cytoplasmic filaments that are connected to the silica spicules.

Glass sponges were more common in the past than they are now, and at one time formed extensive reefs worldwide. Today only one reef of glass sponges survives, and it is located in the Pacific Ocean off the coast of western Canada. Figure 3.3 shows all the world's oceans. In water that varies from 541.3 to 787.4 feet (165 to 240 m) deep, this sponge reef covers about 270.2 square miles (700 km²). The reef is built on deep furrows in the seafloor that were cut by glaciers when sea levels were lower, about 13,000 years ago. The impressive sponge reefs are tall and steep-sided, many reaching heights of 68.9 feet (21 m).

Three species of glass sponges are responsible for building a reef structure: *Heterochone calyx, Aphrocallistes vastus,* and *Farrea occa. Heterochone calyx,* a white to yellow colored organism, grows in a funnel shape up to 4.9 feet (1.5 m) tall. Fingerlike protrusions on the sponge are open-ended and hollow. The smaller *Aphrocallistes vastus* also has protrusions, but they are shaped more like mittens than fingers. *Farrea occa* is a branching, tubular sponge that can form large structures, some up to 49.2 feet (15 m) wide. All three of these reef-building glass sponges are able to secure themselves to firm substrates, like rocks or skeletons of dead sponges, with a basal plate. As they grow, the skeletons of individual sponges fuse together, forming a strong network support system. Several species of non-reef-forming glass sponges grow among them.

The glass sponge reef grows in an area where currents are strong. As fast-moving water flows over the protruding sponge structures, it slows down and deposits some of its load of sediment and organic matter. The organic matter provides nutrients for the sponges, and the sediment builds mounds around them. Some sediment mounds reach heights of 62.3 feet (19 m) and span widths of several kilometers.

Cnidarians

Cnidarians are animals that are characterized by simple, sack-like bodies that are equipped with stinging cells. Some of the most familiar cnidarians are jellyfish, but the group also includes hydrozoans, sea fans, corals, and (as seen in the photo) anemones. Animals in this group have either a bell-shaped medusa or a vase-shaped polyp body plan, as shown in Figure 3.6. Jellyfish demonstrate the medusa, while anemones and corals are polyps. The life cycles of some species of cnidarians include both the polyp and medusa stages.

Cnidarians are slightly more complex than sponges. Their body walls are made of two layers, the epidermis and endodermis, with a jellylike mesoglea between them. The only body opening, the mouth, is responsible for taking in food and expelling wastes. Rings of tentacles, varying in number and length by species, surround the mouth. Each coral animal is crowned with a cluster of short tentacles. A simple network of nerves run through cnidarian bodies, extending to specialized cells called *cnidocytes* that are located in the tentacles. Used in defense and in capturing food, each cnidocyte is armed with a *nematocyst,* a barb attached to a long filament.

Fig. 3.5 Strawberry anemones can be found attached to rocks in clear water. (Courtesy of the Sanctuary Collection, NOAA)

Cnidarian Body Plans

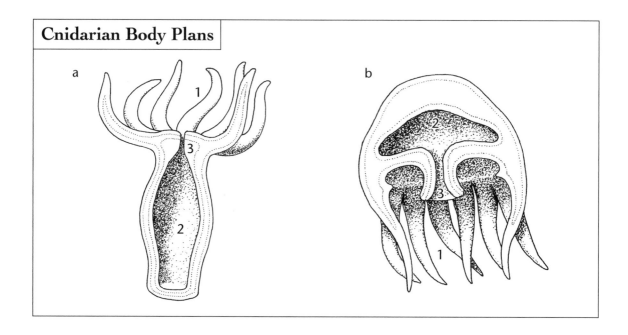

Fig. 3.6 Cnidarians have two body plans, a vase-shaped polyp (a) and a bell-shaped medusa (b). Each body plan is equipped with tentacles (1), a gastrovascular cavity (2), and a single body opening, the mouth (3).

When triggered, the nematocyst uncoils and shoots out its barbed tip. In some species, the tips contain poisons that can paralyze or kill prey, and in others, they are covered with sticky mucus. Once an item is snared, tentacles move it through the cnidarian's mouth and into the gastrovascular cavity.

The polyps of anemones are shaped like columns with distinct tops and bottoms. The upper end of the polyp is the oral disk, made up of a mouth surrounded by tentacles, shown in the upper color insert on page C-2. The opposite end, or basal disk, acts like a suction cup to hold the animal to the substrate. Anemones are not highly mobile but are capable of sliding on their basal disks, or somersaulting on their tentacles from place to place. They can also fill their bodies with air, float to the water's surface, and travel to a new location.

Reproduction in anemones occurs sexually and asexually. In the sexual phase, egg and sperm are released and fertilization occurs in the gastric cavity of the female. The young emerge through the female's mouth as free-swimming larvae. After a short time in the plankton, larvae settle to the bottom

to grow into adult anemones. Asexual reproduction occurs by longitudinal fission, a process in which the organism splits down the middle to form two separate individuals.

Many species of anemones host photosynthetic, symbiotic protists in their tissues. By living together, both the anemone and its one-celled guests benefit. Since they can photosynthesize, the symbionts provide food and oxygen for their host. The anemone, in return, protects the protists from predators and provides a place to live that gets plenty of exposure to sunlight.

One common shelf anemone is the giant green anemone, which can grow to almost one foot (30 cm) in height and nine inches (25 cm) in diameter. The column of this colossal species varies from green to brown, and its tentacles are green, blue, or white. The strawberry anemone (*Corynactis californica*) is smaller and grows in colonies that look like

Fig. 3.7 Each tiny coral animal is a polyp whose mouth is surrounded by tentacles. (Courtesy of Brent Deuel, the Sanctuary Collection, NOAA)

bright red clusters. The northern red anemone (*Telia* [Urticina] *crassicornis*) can be found in sublittoral waters off the northern coasts of both the Pacific and Atlantic Oceans. Usually red, but sometimes mottled with green spots, the anemone grows five inches (12.7 cm) tall. The 100 short, thick tentacles surrounding the northern red anemone's mouth are marked with light-colored rings.

Tube anemones, which are about five inches (12.7 cm) long, live inside mucous tubes made from their own secretions. From the safety of their tubes, the anemones extend their tentacles to catch prey but quickly pull them back inside if startled. The burrowing tube anemone (*Cerianthus aestuani*) lives on the deeper parts of the continental shelf.

The daisy anemone (*Cereus pedunculatus*) is a resident of sublittoral waters to depths of 164 feet (50 m). The dark, trumpet-shaped column of the daisy anemone reaches 4.7 inches (12 cm) in height. Numerous short, banded tentacles, varying in number from 500 to 1,000, surround the mouth.

Like anemones, corals are small animals that spend their lives in the polyp stage. Those classified as hard corals secrete protective skeletons around themselves, while the soft corals do not. Both kinds are found in several locations on continental shelves and form dense populations on coral reefs. Hard corals are the architects of coral reefs and are responsible for building the structures that create the reef environments.

The number and variety of hard and soft corals is staggering. In shallow, tropical reefs, elkhorn coral (*Acropora palmate*), staghorn coral (*Acropora cervicornis*), shown in Figure 3.8, and finger coral (*Porites compressa*) closely resemble their namesakes. Boulder coral (*Montastrea annularis*) creates rocklike mounds up to 10 feet (3.05 m) high, while yellow porous coral (*Porites astreoides*) looks like small, bright yellow boulders with bumpy surfaces. Common brain coral (*Diploria strigosa*) is a medium-sized hemisphere grooved with ridges and valleys that resemble brain matter.

Corals are not restricted to shallow, tropical waters. Off the coast of Florida, *Oculina varicosa* forms coral banks in water 164.04 to 328.08 feet (50 to 100 m) deep, near the edge of the continental shelf. A slow-growing, branching, ivory-colored

specimen, *Oculina* can form mounds up to 98.4 feet (30 m) in height. The northern stony coral (*Astrangia danae*), found off the southeastern coast of the United States, is a temperate water species that grows as crusts on rocks and other firm surfaces.

Several types of corals occur in even colder waters, thriving where temperatures range from 39°F to 52°F (4°C to 13°C). Cold water corals may be found from 131.2 to 20,669.3 feet (40 to 6,300 m) on the edges of the continental shelves and in fjords. Often living too deep to receive any sunlight, these corals lack the zooxanthellae that are characteristic of their tropical cousins. The white coral, *Lophelia*, forms several cold water reefs around the world. The largest covers about 38.6 square miles (100 km²) off the coast of Norway.

Another group of cnidarians, the octocorals, also forms colonies. The individual polyps resemble anemones, but the animals live in colonies that are surrounded by a tough

Fig. 3.8 Staghorn corals can be found in beds of sea grass. (Courtesy of Florida Keys National Marine Sanctuary, NOAA)

matrix. Dead man's fingers (*Alcyonium digitatum*) is an octo-coral that varies in color from white to pink to orange, and is characterized by fleshy lobes and fingerlike projections. The four- to eight-inch (10- to 20-cm) colonies attach to stone and shells. The sea whip (*Leptogorgia virgulata*) forms colonies of slender, whiplike branches that can be purple, tan, or red. A similar species, *Lophogorgia hebes,* may appear in shades of purple, red, tan, or orange. *Octocorallia* is an octo-coral that usually grows in dense colonies in cold water reefs.

Corals spend their entire adult lives in the polyp phase, but hydroids are a group of cnidarians that exist as both polyps and medusae during their life cycles. Hydrozoids form colonies that look like delicate branches or fern fronds. Within the colony, individual polyps specialize, dividing the labor needed to support the group. Some individuals are in charge of reproduction, some feeding, and others defense. All the polyps in a hydrozoan colony are connected with a shared gastrovascular cavity. Colonies are usually very small and can be found attached to surfaces like rocks. The animals within a hydroid colony are tiny, measuring about 0.04 inches (one mm) in width. Many species support autotrophic zooxanthel-lae in their tissues. Like anemones, hydroids can also capture prey with stinging tentacles.

The bottlebrush hydroid (*Thuiaria thuja*) looks very much like the brush for which it was named. Each bottlebrush colony has a strong central stem surrounded by short branch-es of the same length. Found in all depths of continental shelf waters, the bottlebrush is gray in color. The sea fir hydroid (*Sertularia*) forms delicate stems that support flattened, branched colonies. These small hydroids are usually smaller than 11.8 inches (30 cm) and thrive in shallow areas where water is very energetic.

Bottlebrushes and sea firs are sessile animals, but two types of hydroids are free-floating species. The by-the-wind sailor (*Velella*) resembles a small jellyfish but is actually a colony of individual hydrozoans that are supported in the water by an inflated blue sail. As drifters, by-the-wind sailors blow across the continental shelf waters, open sea waters, and sometimes into intertidal zones. Within the colony, each animal, or zooid, has a specific job. Zooids of *Velella* that are equipped with food tentacles capture small fish, fish eggs, and insect-like copepods that are floating in the plankton.

The Portuguese man-of-war is another colonial hydrozoid that spends its life floating at the sea's surface. A gas-filled, iridescent blue bladder, measuring 12 inches (30 cm) tall and six inches (15 cm) high, buoys up the colony. Three kinds of polyps hang below the bladder, dangling tentacles that can grow to lengths of 60 feet (18 m). Potent toxins in the nematocysts of these tentacles can seriously injure people and kill small animals.

Jellyfish are individual cnidarians that spend their lives in the medusa stage. Hundreds of species float in the continental shelf waters searching for food. *Aequorea* are small organisms,

Associations with Jellyfish

Even though jellyfish do not form colonies like corals and hydroids, individuals are rarely alone. Several other types of animals "hitchhike" on jellyfish. Most of the hitchhikers neither help nor harm the jellies, forming relationships that are described as commensal. A few are parasites that cause life-threatening damage.

Several types of juvenile and larval fish, as well as adult medusafish (*Icichthys lockingtoni*), Pacific butterfish (*Peprilus simillimus*), and walleye pollock (*Theragra chalcoramma*), swim alongside of jellyfish. When they are threatened, these fish hide in the veils of hanging tentacles. Scientists are not sure why the jellyfish do not sting these shy fish. Some speculate that the fish are able to avoid the dangerous stinging tips of the tentacles, but others think that the fish either develop immunity to their toxins or coat their bodies with mucus that the toxins cannot penetrate.

In other cases, jellyfish are preyed on or parasitized by hitchhikers. During their larval phases, some species of crabs stay close to jellyfish and steal their kills, depriving the jellies of their food. At times, these larval crabs even nibble on the flesh of the jellyfish, harming, but rarely killing, them. In addition, insect-like amphipods dig pits in the jellyfishes' flesh where they embed themselves. From these stations, the amphipods are protected from predators and are in positions to share the food captured by their hosts.

ranging from 3.2 to 7.9 inches (8 to 20 cm in diameter). Like most jellies, *Aequorea* are virtually colorless and difficult to detect in the water. They are sometimes spotted as they bioluminesce along their margins, briefly showing a soft, bluish color.

A sea nettle, *Chrysaora fuscescens,* is known to many swimmers because of its painful sting. Long white and maroon tentacles trail below its brown bell, which is 11.8 inches (30 cm) in diameter. Purple-striped jellyfish (*Chrysaora colorata*), in the lower color insert on page C-2, are larger than sea nettles, with bells up to three feet (0.9 m) in diameter. Their white and purple bells are easy to spot near the water's surface when these jellyfish are feeding on plankton.

Worms

Worms live alongside sponges, anemones, and corals on the floor of the continental shelf. Worms are more complex than both sponges and cnidarians. Based on their body structure, they are divided into several groups, the largest three of which are flatworms, roundworms, and segmented worms.

Tissue-thin and flattened in shape, flatworms are animals that lack appendages and segments. The one-way digestive system of a flatworm shows through its translucent body wall. To feed, a flatworm extends a muscular tube, the pharynx, onto its meal. The tube secretes digestive enzymes which liquefy the food, enabling the worm to suck up its meal through the pharynx. Most species prey on protozoans and small invertebrates.

Flatworms may divide asexually by fission to produce two identical offspring, or they can undergo sexual reproduction. In some populations, all the worms are females who lay eggs that develop without fertilization. More commonly, flatworms are hermaphrodites, animal having both male and female reproductive organs. To fertilize eggs, two worms cross-fertilize, each injecting the other with sperm.

Because they are soft and slow-moving, flatworms might be easy targets for some predators. To avoid being eaten, some species have developed camouflaging coloration, making it difficult for their predators to find them. Others are brightly colored, an adaptation that advertises danger or distastefulness. A few nonpoisonous species mimic the coloration of poisonous animals, taking advantage of their dangerous reputations.

The candy striped flatworm (*Prostheceraeus vittatus*) spends most of its time hiding under stones and rubble. Colored bright yellow, the worm has dark stripes that run from head to tail. The candy striped flatworm travels by crawling across the seafloor using cilia on the underside of its body, or by swimming with an undulating motion.

Bdelloura candida is a white flatworm that attaches to the undersides of horseshoe crabs, clinging to their gills with a specially adapted suction disc. The worms appear to ride along with the horseshoe crabs without parasitizing them. On the other hand, *Polydora robi,* a passenger on hermit crabs, is not as easy to live with. *Polydora robi* burrows into the shell of its host and feeds on the eggs. In hermit crabs that produce only small egg caches, the worm can significantly damage reproductive potential.

The roundworms, or nematodes, are much smaller and less conspicuous than flatworms. Most are transparent and so small that they are barely visible to the naked eye. Despite their small size, populations of roundworms are large, up to 1 million individuals per 1.2 square yards (one m²) of sediment, making them important members of the bottom-dwelling community. Nematodes live in the spaces between soil particles in the sediment where they feed on algae or consume bits of organic material.

There are more than 4,000 species of marine nematodes; a single handful of sand can yield up to 20 different species. Some species lay down mucus trails, then glide on the trails from one sand particle to another. Other species use mucus to glue their bodies to sand particles or to glue sand particles together into tiny balls, possibly forming mini-environments for themselves.

The segmented worms, or annelids, are larger than roundworms and flatworms, some reaching lengths of several inches. The bodies of annelids are divided into sections or segments.

In the marine environment, most annelids fall in the subgroup polychaete, worms that have fleshy extensions called parapodia on each segment. Parapodia contain the worm's gills and are associated with stiff bristles called *setae*. During reproduction, male and female polychaetes release gametes into the water, where they unite to form zygotes. Zygotes grow into larvae that swim in the plankton before settling to the seafloor. Depending on the species, polychaetes may prey on other animals, or feed on organic matter suspended in the water or found in the sediment.

Polychaetes exhibit one of two lifestyles: free-living or tube-dwelling. The free-living, or errant, species wander on the seafloor searching for food, then return to a tube or burrow to rest. Errant worms have long slender bodies that look about the same from head to tail. The head may have some

Worm Comparisons

Segmented worms are much more advanced and complex than flatworms. The digestive systems of flatworms are one-way tubes sandwiched between two body walls. However, segmented worms have a space between their two body walls called the body cavity, or coelom, that represents an important evolutionary advance, one that provides a place for the body's internal organs. In segmented worms, organs are held in their proper places inside the coelom by a membrane, the peritoneum.

All animals with coeloms are equipped with one set of muscles around the body wall and another set around the digestive system. The body wall muscles help the animal move about, while the digestive system muscles push food along the digestive tract. In contrast, flatworms have only one set of muscles in their body wall, and these muscles must carry out both functions.

Segmentation is an advance in animal evolution because segmented animals can increase in size by adding more body portions. In addition, segments can become specialized to carry out certain jobs. Flatworms are therefore limited in size as well as in the degree of specialization they can reach because they lack segments.

A flatworm gets oxygen and loses carbon dioxide by simple diffusion through the epidermis. Segmented worms have more complex gas exchange systems. Oxygen diffuses through the skin into blood vessels. Blood then carries oxygen to cells deep in specialized structures for breathing and feeding, including strong jaws and a tubular feeding organ called a proboscis. Examples of errant species include scale worms, sea mice, blood worms, and clam worms.

Pontogenia indica is one of several species of worms known as sea mice. Living on muddy bottoms, these plump worms dig through the soil, where they feed on detritus and protists. The worms' bodies are covered with short, hairlike spines that are poisonous and good predator deterrents.

Blood worms (*Glycera*) have pale skin through which their red body fluid can be seen. An active animal, a blood worm burrows in sand or muddy substrates with its proboscis, which is armed with four small, black fangs. Blood worms are found preying on small invertebrates at all depths of the continental shelf.

the worm's body, while it picks up carbon dioxide and carries it out of the body. The blood of segmented worms contains hemoglobin, an iron-containing compound that attracts oxygen and binds to it. Blood with hemoglobin is capable of carrying 50 times more oxygen than blood that lacks the molecule. Near the head of the segmented worm, five pairs of muscular vessels or hearts squeeze rhythmically to keep blood circulating through the worm's body.

Segmented worms have much more advanced digestive systems than flatworms do. A flatworm has one opening, a mouth, for food and wastes. A segmented worm has two openings, a mouth at one end and an anus at the other. The mouth opens to an esophagus that leads to a muscular pharynx.

Food travels from the pharynx to the crop where it can be stored temporarily before entering the gizzard, an organ that grinds it. From there, food goes to the intestine, the site of digestion. Digested nutrients enter the bloodstream, and waste materials are expelled through the anus. Segmented worms also have special organs called nephridia that remove nitrogen wastes from blood and excrete those wastes through tiny openings in the body wall.

The evolutionary advancements from flatworms to segmented worms are reflected in other animals such as mollusks and crustaceans, as well as in vertebrates. The segmented worms, although still evolutionarily simple, provided the groundwork from which further advancement evolved.

Paralepidonotus ampulliferus and *Iphione muricata* are two species of polychaetes that are described as scale worms, named for the enlarged scales on their dorsal sides. These slow-moving animals feed on small invertebrates. Scale worms often share space with anemones, coral, and other animals in commensal relationships. Clam worms (*Nereis*) are not scaled but have well-developed parapodia and head appendages. These polychaetes may have four or more pairs of tentacle-like extensions on their heads. During the day, they hide in mucus-lined sand burrows, but at night they emerge to find prey, like small crustaceans or mollusks, or to scavenge on dead animals.

Tube-dwelling polychaetes are sedentary, spending all their time in one place waiting for food to come to them. Sedentary worms are shorter than errant species, and their bodies are divided into distinct regions. Because these worms spend their lives inside tubes or holes, they have specially adapted appendages for feeding and breathing. Most feed on plankton or small organic material suspended in the water, although a few catch prey.

Lumbrineris, is a tube-dwelling polychaete that burrows in soft-bottom sediments throughout the continental shelf. *Lumbrineris* uses powerful jaws to grasp its food, which may be prey or dead organic matter, depending on the species. *Cirratulus cirratulus* also buries in sediment, leaving only gills and feeding extensions called palps, above the soil. Bamboo worms (*Clymenella*) are aptly named, for they look very much like four-inch (10 cm) lengths of bamboo. Each worm's body is made up of only a few long segments with very few parapodia. From their sand- or mud-encrusted tubes, bamboo worms consume mud to get the nutrients it contains.

The brightly colored tentacles of one tube-dwelling sabellid worm has earned it two nicknames: feather duster and fanworm. From the safety of its tube, the fanworm spreads its tentacles in wide, fan-shaped arches to gather bits of food and to exchange gases. The tubes of fanworms are lined with mucus and covered with mud and sand.

Honeycomb worms build tusk-shaped tubes that they attach to substrates like rocks or shells. Over time, colonies of honeycomb worms can expand into reeflike structures. The serpulids, or plume worms, are named for the frilly plume extending from their tubes. Like other tube worms, the plumes are designed for food gathering and gas exchange. Tubes of serpulids differ from those of most other worms. Instead of being open at both ends so that water can circulate freely, serpulids build blind tubes and must draw water in, and expel it, from the same opening.

Conclusion

The continental shelves, with their relatively shallow waters and vast expanses of nutrient-rich sediments, are home to hundreds of species of sponges, cnidarians, and worms. The simplest animals are the sponges, which spend their lives attached to firm substrates at all depths of the seafloor. Like other filter-feeders, sponges require nutrient-rich water, so they compete with algae and shellfish for the best locations. A few species expand their territories by living on the shells of snails and hermit crabs. To avoid competition for space, some make their homes in water that is too deep and dark to support algae.

Sponges may have skeletons made of calcium carbonate, protein, or silica particles. Those made of silica are called the glass sponges. In the past, these animals built extensive reef systems in cold, deep waters. Today only one glass sponge reef exists, and it is found off the west coast of Canada.

Cnidarians make up a large part of the invertebrate population on the continental shelf. All cnidarians possess stinging cells that they use in defense and to capture food. Many cnidarians, including anemones, corals, and hydroids, live attached to substrates. To feed, the cnidarians open their mouths and wave feeding tentacles to snare prey. In shallow water, some species contain zooxanthellae, green protists that produce food for the cnidarians. Jellyfish and a few hydroids float through the water, dangling the tentacles in search of food.

Worms outnumber both sponges and cnidarians on the continental shelf. The simplest worms are flatworms, whose thin bodies house one-way digestive systems. Flatworms may be free-living, parasitic, or commensal. Some of the free-living species are poisonous, a quality they advertise with bright colors. Nematodes, or roundworms, a group of organisms so small they can barely be seen with the naked eye, live between soil particles. Most feed on organic matter and play key roles in nutrient recycling. Polychaetes are segmented worms that live on, or in, the sediments. Errant polychaetes are free-living animals that wander in search of food. Sedentary polychaetes build tubes of mucus and sand, catching their food with tentacles that they wave above the soil surface.

Mollusks, Crustaceans, Echinoderms, and Tunicates
The Most Common Animals on the Continental Shelf

4

Simple invertebrates, such as sponges, cnidarians, and worms, make up only a portion of the marine invertebrates. Several other types of animals, the mollusks, crustaceans, and echinoderms, are more advanced. These groups include such familiar sea life as clams, whelks, horseshoe crabs, shrimp, crabs, sea stars, and sea cucumbers. Living among the invertebrates are tunicates. Commonly known as sea squirts, tunicates are the simplest chordates, organisms with nerve cords, and are evolutionarily more advanced than the invertibrates.

The organization of tissues, organs, and organ systems of advanced invertebrates give them a level of complexity not reached in the more primitive types. Simple organisms absorb oxygen directly into their cells from the environment. In structurally complex animals, many of the cells are too far from the environment to meet their gas exchange needs. The bodies of these marine animals require sophisticated respiratory systems that include gills.

Gills are respiratory organs that serve as the sites of gas exchange in aquatic organisms. The tissues of gills are thin and packed with thousands of tiny blood vessels. Gill tissues are highly folded, making it possible to crowd a large surface area into a small space. As water flows over gills, oxygen that is dissolved in it diffuses into the bloodstream. At the same time, carbon dioxide dissolved in the blood diffuses into the water.

The body of a complex invertebrate has a circulatory system to deliver oxygen and pick up carbon dioxide at each of its millions of cells. The circulatory system also delivers nutrient molecules, which are processed and prepared by the digestive system, and picks up waste products, taking them to the excretory system. All these body systems are run and coordinated by the nervous system, which is centralized on the anterior end of the animal.

Mollusks

Mollusks are members of a large group of organisms that contains more than 112,000 species, second in number only to the arthropods. Animals that are mollusks vary radically in size, shape, and lifestyles. Despite their differences, all mollusks share several common characteristics. Each has a soft body, the characteristic described by the Latin term from which their name is derived, *mollusca*. The bodies of mollusks contain organ systems for circulation, respiration, reproduction, digestion, and excretion. In addition, each mollusk body is covered with a thin tissue called the mantle. In some species the mantle secretes the shell and one or more defensive chemicals, like ink, mucus, or acid. A mollusk also possesses a muscular foot that is used for locomotion, whether it be swimming, digging, or crawling. Except for organisms in the subgroup called bivalves, mollusks feed by scraping up food with a filelike tongue, the *radula,* which can efficiently take in algae, animal tissue, or detritus. A bivalve is a filter feeder that traps and consumes food particles suspended in water.

In mollusks, sexes are separate. Bivalves release their eggs and sperm into the water, and fertilization occurs there. In other types of mollusks, sperm are transferred into the body of the female, and fertilization takes place internally. Fertilized females deposit strings or cases of eggs on the sand, seaweed, or rocks. In both internal and external fertilization, zygotes develop into swimming larvae that metamorphose into adult forms.

Some mollusks have hard, external shells that protect their soft internal organs. The presence, or absence, of a shell is one of several characteristics used to classify mollusks that live on the continental shelf into three groups: gastropods, bivalves, and cephalopods.

Gastropods

In the waters of the continental shelf, gastropods make up the largest and probably best known group of mollusks. Gastropods include snails, whelks, limpets, and nudibranchs. The term gastropod literally means "stomach foot" and refers to the central location of a muscular foot that gastropods depend on for locomotion. Most gastropods have one shell, although a group called the nudibranchs are shell-less. In some species, an *operculum,* a flap or door that can close the shell, protects the occupant from danger. The head of a gastropod is equipped with sensory organs including light-sensitive dots, tentacles, and a mouth.

Snails are slow-moving mollusks whose bodies are protected by spiral shells and, in many species, thin opercula. On the continental shelf, snails occupy many niches. The top shells (*Gibbula*) climb up and down kelp stalks, eating as they go. The pheasant snails (*Phaesianella australis*) graze on smaller types of algae in water that is knee-deep. The New Zealand screw shell snails (*Maoricolpus roseus*) feed on organic matter suspended in the water, and prefer sand or shell bottoms from depths of 9.8 to 164.0 feet (3 to 50 m). Found in shallow water on continental shelves from Alaska to Baja California, the purple olive snails (*Olivella biplicata*) have smooth, glossy shells.

Limpets are close relatives of snails that have cone-shaped shells that are not coiled. Some species, such as the blue-rayed limpet (*Helcion pelludicum*), graze on kelp blades. Larvae of blue-rayed limpets dig cavities in the kelps' holdfasts, weakening their grip on the seafloor and increasing the likelihood that the entire plant will wash away during a storm. As a result, the burrows of these larvae have a significant impact on the size, and maturity, of kelp stands.

Abalones, a group of snails with flattened shells, are harvested commercially for food. An average-size specimen is about 11.8 in (30 cm) long and can be found clinging to firm surfaces with its strong, muscular foot. Abalones use their sharp radulae to scrap algae from rocks. Most feed in the safety of crevices or under ledges, avoiding open areas where they might be targets for predators. The black abalone (*Haliotis cracherodii*) is a west coast resident that lives in sublittoral regions, generally in 20 feet (6.1 m) of water. The flat abalone (*Haliotis walallensis*), whose shell is yellow and brown with a pebble texture, is found in water up to 70 feet (21.3m) deep.

Whelks are large snails that prey on mussels, clams, and their relatives. A whelk uses the thick lip of its own shell to pry open the two shells of a bivalve, then inserts its proboscis and feeds. Most whelks hunt during the day, moving slowly across the seafloor. The knobbed whelk (*Busycon carica*) is often seen searching for meals in the sublittoral zone. When water temperatures become either extremely warm or extremely cold, groups of whelks may migrate into deeper shelf waters.

Conches are large snails, like whelks, but instead of preying on other animals, they eat algae. To feed, a conch sucks up its meals with its tubular proboscis. The shells of conches are heavy and the rims form thick, flaring lips. One of the largest species, the queen conch (*Strombus gigas*) grows to one foot (30 cm) in length. The territorial Florida fighting conch (*Strombus alatus*) is smaller, measuring about three inches (7.5 cm) long.

Gastropods that lack shells, the nudibranchs, are some of the most colorful marine invertebrates. The name nudibranch literally means naked (nudi) gills (branchia) and refers to the fact that the gills of these animals are not covered with shells. Some are equipped with appendages on their backs called cerata that act as supplemental gills. Known also as sea slugs, the nudibranchs are not equipped with proboscises, so they feed with radulae and jaws.

The orange-tipped nudibranch (*Triopha catalinae*) lives in sublittoral waters to depths of 110 feet (34 m). Reaching lengths of six inches (15 cm) and widths of 0.75 inches (1.9 cm), this wormlike gastropod is white with bright orange spots. On the rear portion of its body are five feathery gills and several orange antennae. Two hornlike projections on the top of its head are sensory organs.

Although they look very much like nudibranchs, sea hares are a separate group of gastropods. They are differentiated by the presence of small internal shells and a flap of skin that protects the gills. Wide, winglike extensions of a sea hare's foot, as well as tall antennae on its head, give the animal a harelike appearance. Most species, like the spotted sea hare (*Aplysia dactylomela*) and Willcox's sea hare (*Aplysia willcoxi*), are herbivores that can be found crawling or swimming among seaweed.

Bivalves

Bivalves are mollusks whose soft body parts are covered by two shells, or valves, that hinge together on one side. Strong adductor muscles attach to the inside surfaces of the shells to open and close them. Clams, mussels, scallops, and abalones are a few of the bivalves found on the continental shelf.

A bivalve, like the one shown in Figure 4.1, extends a large foot from the center of its body through partially opened shells. Depending on the species, the foot may attach to a substrate or burrow into the sand. Burrowing species possess two siphons, tubes that extend from the body to transport water to and from the gills, which are located in the mantle cavity. In filter-feeding bivalves, gills have two functions: to exchange gases and to gather food. As water flows over the gills, hairlike cilia and mucus trap bits of food and move them toward the mouth.

Hundreds of species of clams are found on the continental shelf. Razor clams (*Ensis directus*) live from the shoreline to waters as deep as 120 feet (36.6 m). The shells of razor clams are long and thin, and grow to lengths of 10 inches (25.4 cm). Burrowed in the sediment, these animals filter diatoms, zooplankton, and organic matter from the water that they pull over their gills. The Pacific littleneck clam (*Protothaca staminea*) has rounded shells, often marked with brown zigzag patterns. Found on sandy bottoms from the water's edge to depths of 59.1 feet (18 m), Pacific littleneck clams can burrow 3.9 inches (10 cm) deep.

Fig. 4.1   A clam is a mollusk whose body is protected by two valves. Water is circulated over the gills through incurrent and excurrent siphons. In this illustration, the right valve partially covers the muscular foot, which is used for locomotion.

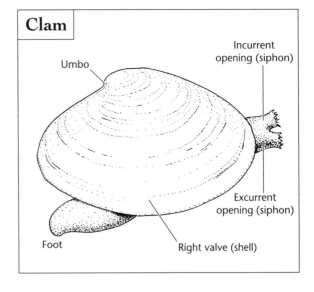

Scallops differ from most bivalves in that they lie on the surface of the sand instead of burrowed in it, and they lack the typical gastropod foot. As suspension feeders, scallops pull water into their shells and pass it over their food-gathering gills. The kelp scallop (*Leptopecten latiauratus*), a gray to brownish-green species that is covered in white zigzag lines, lives on rocks, kelps, and other firm substrates in water up to 150 feet (45.7) deep. The great scallop (*Pecten maximus*), which can grow to 5.9 inches (15 cm), prefers sandy substrates in water as deep as 328.1 feet (100 m).

Another bivalve that lives on top of the sand, the mussel, attaches to rocks or other solid substrates. Blue mussels (*Mytilus edulis*) have shells that are black externally and blue on the inside surfaces. To secure its body in place in energetic shallow waters, a blue mussel secretes tough byssal threads from a gland in its foot. Showing little preference for one substrate over the other, mussels form extensive colonies in waters from shore to 49.2 feet (15 m).

As a group, bivalves are long-lived animals. Scientists have recently concluded that the ages of bivalves can be accurately determined by counting the growth ridges on their shells, very much like counting the rings of a tree. Depending on the species, life spans vary from a couple of years to a couple of centuries. Recent ring counts reveal that the most common bivalve in Canadian waters, *Spisula solidissima,* has an average span of 17 years. The soft-shell or steamer clam (*Mya arenaria*) often survives nearly 30 years. The geoduck (*Panopea generosa*) of the West Coast of the United States, and the *Crenomytilus grayanus* from the Peter the Great Bay, an inlet of the Sea of Japan on the eastern shore of Russia, show up to 120 growth rings. A specimen found in the middle of the continental shelf in the Atlantic Ocean displays 220 rings. That means that some of the bivalves alive today were around before the U.S. Constitution was written.

Cephalopods

Cephalopods, or the head-footed animals, are so named because the structures that propel them through the water are located near their heads. Lacking the typical mollusk-style foot, the locomotive structures in cephalopods are modified as tentacles. Cephalopods on the continental shelf include octopus, squid, and cuttlefish. All are accomplished predators that use their suction-cup armed tentacles to snare prey. Tentacles then push food items into the animals' beaklike mouths, which are well-designed for killing and tearing off tissue.

One of a cephalopod's most distinguishing characteristics is its advanced nervous system. With the largest invertebrate brain, a cephalopod is capable of processing information and learning new things. Much of the information coming into the cephalopod brain arrives through well-developed eyes. The tentacles, which are sensitive touch receptors and capable of distinguishing chemicals in the water, also provide the cephalopod with information about the environment.

Cephalopod Camouflage

Cephalopods are soft bodied and have no external shells to protect them, so they are easy prey for hungry hunters like fish, sharks, and seals. Defense strategies used by cephalopods include techniques in camouflage that enable them to alter both the color and texture of their skin. As a cephalopod moves across the seafloor looking for food, the color of its skin changes almost instantly. This remarkable ability is mediated by the animal's advanced nervous system.

If startled, a cephalopod's eyes relay messages to the body telling it to go into a defensive mode. The eyes take in the color of the surroundings, then send nerve impulses to special skin cells called chromatophores that contain bags of pigment. When the bags expand, the color becomes intense; when they contract, the color fades to tiny dots. Camouflage is achieved by expansion of some chromatophores and contraction of others.

If there was a contest to judge the most creative use of chromatophores, the mimic octopus would win. The repertoire of this master of camouflage includes sea snakes, lionfish, and other poisonous animals. To imitate a lionfish, the cephalopod turns blue and flares its legs to look like poisonous fins. To impersonate a sea snake, the octopus changes its colors to yellow and black bands, tucks its body and all but two legs into a hole, then waves the two exposed legs in snake-like fashion.

Cephalopods have two strategies for avoiding predators: confusion and camouflage. Most species release ink that acts like a smokescreen to confuse predators and permit a quick escape. The ink of some species deadens the sense of smell of their predators while the ink of other species contains bioluminescent bacteria. Cephalopods can also adjust their body color to blend in with almost any environment.

As a general rule, octopuses are small, measuring less than 11.8 inches (30 cm) in diameter. When searching for food, an octopus crawls on its eight tentacles or arms on the seafloor. If startled or threatened, the octopus may jet forward by using its water propulsion system, sucking water into a muscular sac located in the mantle cavity, then forcefully expelling it out a narrow siphon. Many octopuses build lairs or dens where they rest during the day, and where females lay and *brood* their eggs. The entrances of dens are often marked with piles, or middens, of the shells and exoskeletons of their prey.

The brown or gray common octopus (*Octopus vulgaris*) is difficult to detect on a rocky seafloor because its body is so well camouflaged. The red octopus (*Octopus rubescens*) ranges in color from red to brown, green, or yellow, depending on its environment. The giant octopus (*Octopus dofleini*) is larger than its cousins, generally weighing from 22.1 to 33.1 pounds (10 to 15 kg). The skin of a giant octopus is smooth and brown when the animal is at rest, but can change colors when it feels threatened.

Squid are swimming cephalopods that rely on their water propulsion system to propel them through the seas. The oval-shaped body of a squid, shown in Figure 4.2, has two fins, eight arms, and two tentacles. Internally, a squid contains a strip of hard protein, a pen, which gives support to the mantle. *Loligo opalescens* is a small species, reaching diameters of only 6.3 inches (16 cm). *Loligo forbesi* and *Loligo vulgaris* are much bigger species that live in continental shelf waters of the Atlantic. The Caribbean reef squid (*Sepioteuthis sepioidea*) has large fins and resembles a cuttlefish. The giant squid (*Architeutis dux*), the largest of all invertebrates, lives in the deep parts of the oceans but swims up to the continental shelf at night to feed. Scientists have never seen a living specimen, but research on dead ones suggests an average size of 60 feet (18 m).

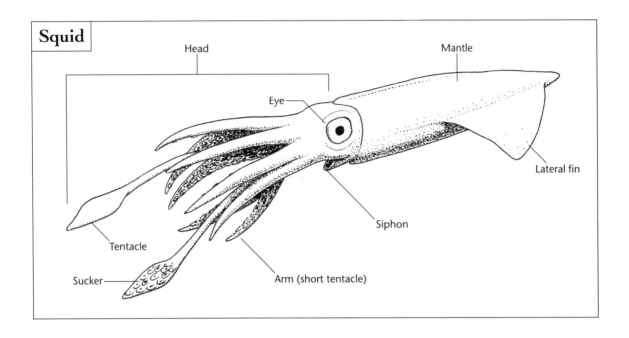

Cuttlefish are cephalopods with reduced, internal bones called cuttlebones. With eight arms and two tentacles, a cuttlefish swims and feeds very much like squid. The common cuttlefish (*Sepia officinalis*) has a brown to green color, while *Sepioloidea lineolata*, an Australian species, is white with black stripes. The largest species in the world is the giant Australian cuttlefish (*Sepia pharaonis*), which can weigh 11 pounds (5 kg).

Arthropods

Arthropods are the most successful group of animals on Earth in regards to variety and population size, accounting for 85 percent of the animals. Familiar terrestrial arthropods include the insects and spiders, while some of the marine arthropods living on the continental shelf are shrimp, lobsters, crabs, horseshoe crabs, and sea spiders. In comparison, all of the *vertebrates* (fish, reptiles, birds, and mammals) make up less than 5 percent of the planet's animals. The other 10 percent is made up of other invertebrates, like the mollusks.

An arthropod's body is divided into segments to which several types of appendages are attached. An *appendage* is a leg,

Fig. 4.2 At the head end, the squid's body is equipped with a well-developed eye as well as eight arms and two tentacles, each of which is covered with suckers. Near the eye, a siphon carries water to the gills. The mantle is modified into a body covering with two lateral fins for steering.

Advantages and Disadvantages of an Exoskeleton

More than 80 percent of the animal species are equipped with a hard, outer covering called an exoskeleton. The functions of exoskeletons are similar to those of other types of skeletal systems. Like the internal skeletons (endoskeletons) of amphibians, reptiles, birds, and mammals, exoskeletons support the tissues and give shape to the bodies of invertebrates. Exoskeletons offer some other advantages. Serving as a suit of armor, they are excellent protection against predators. Also, because they completely cover an animal's tissues, exoskeletons prevent them from drying out. In addition, exoskeletons serve as

points of attachment for muscles, providing animals with more leverage and mechanical advantage than an endoskeleton can offer. That is why a tiny shrimp can cut a fish in half with its claw or lift an object 50 times heavier than its own body.

Despite all their good points, exoskeletons have some drawbacks. They are heavy, so the only animals that have been successful with them over time are those that have remained small. In addition, an animal must molt, or shed, its exoskeleton to grow. During and immediately after a molt, an animal is unprotected and vulnerable to predators.

antenna, or other part that extends from a segment of the body. A hard *exoskeleton* protects the body and its vulnerable internal organs. Exoskeletons are primarily composed of *chitin,* a hard, flexible material that is made of chains of molecules.

In most arthropods, sexes are separate. In many species the male deposits sperm in the female's body, where they remain until the eggs leave the ovary. Zygotes that result from the fusion of egg and sperm mature into plankton-swimming larvae that settle to the seafloor to mature.

Crustaceans

The crustaceans, animals such as crabs, shrimp, and lobsters, make up the largest division of arthropods. As shown in Figure 4.3, a typical crustacean has three specialized body sections: head, thorax, and abdomen. The head is equipped with two sets of antennae and three sets of feeding appendages. In some species, one set of feeding appendages

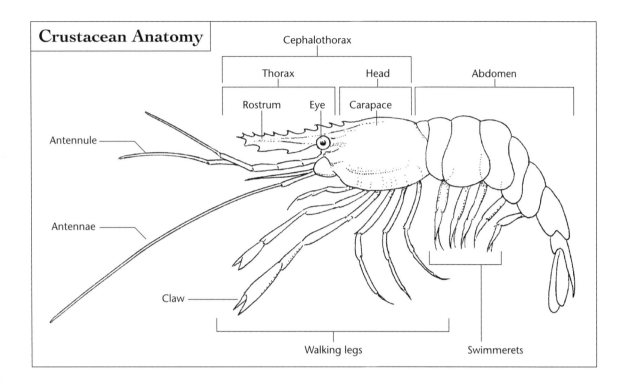

Crustacean Anatomy

Cephalothorax

Thorax   Head   Abdomen

Rostrum   Eye   Carapace

Antennule

Antennae

Claw

Walking legs   Swimmerets

ends in large claws that are capable of exerting hundreds of pounds of pressure. The body and abdomen of a crustacean is equipped with walking or swimming appendages. Sexually, the animals have separate genders, and females are in charge of egg laying and brooding.

Amphipods are tiny crustaceans that may be long and thin or stout and compact. Exhibiting a variety of lifestyles and nutritional strategies, amphipods live in almost all marine habitats, including the continental shelf. Although the majority inhabit the seafloor, a good number are planktonic. Amphipods feed on macroalgae, organic matter in sediment, dead plants and animals, and marine mammals. Whale lice are examples of parasitic amphipods that ride around with whales and eat their skin.

Another group of small crustaceans are the isopods. Closely resembling their terrestrial relatives, the pill bugs and sow bugs, isopods have segmented bodies. Depending on species, the habitats, sizes, and diets of isopods are widely different.

Fig. 4.3 The body of a crustacean is divided into three areas: head, thorax, and abdomen. The head and thorax are fused to form a cephalothorax.

Krill

Despite its frigid temperatures, the Southern Ocean near Antarctica is teeming with life. The food web there is supported by diatoms, which are nourished by upwelling currents that carry nutrients from deep seafloors to surface water. Diatoms provide food for many species of zooplankton, the most numerous of which are tiny crustaceans called krill. Krill, shown in the upper color insert on page C-3, are shrimplike creatures that range from one to two inches (3 to 6 cm) in length.

On the zooplankton scale, krill are large animals whose weight makes it difficult to stay afloat. To prevent sinking, krill swim constantly. Because swimming expends a lot of energy these crustaceans require a tremendous amount of food. To meet this need, krill feed constantly, collecting diatoms by pumping water through net-like combs on their legs.

In the summer, when warm temperatures and long days boost the size of diatom populations, populations of krill soar. In some areas, swarms of krill cover hundreds of meters of sea surface. In the winter, productivity drops to almost zero because of short days and cold temperatures. During this period, krill live in deeper waters and feed on detritus.

Krill are important sources of food for a variety of continental shelf water animals. When productivity is high, whales, birds, fish, squid, and hundreds of other types of organisms travel to the southern waters to feed. Scientists estimate that during a typical summer, fish consume more than 100 million tons of the tiny crustaceans. A blue whale can take in a ton of krill at each feeding, and most blue whales feed four times a day. Krill also makes up almost 80 percent of the diet of seabirds in the region.

Isopods crawl across the sediment, swim in the water column, and cling to plants and animals by their barbed legs.

Excorallana tricornis is an isopod found in waters near Florida and the Caribbean. The sediments of sea grass beds and the thalli of brown algae are its favorite places to live. *Excorallana tricornis* can also be found clinging to the gills of rays and attached to squirrelfish. Other species of isopods parasitize shrimp by attaching to their sides, creating tumorlike swelling and feeding on the blood of their hosts. The isopod that parasitizes grouper attaches to the fish's head, as shown in Figure 4.4.

Shrimp, lobsters, and crabs are larger crustaceans whose first pair of legs is often modified as claws. Shrimp, the smallest of the group, have relatively lightweight exoskeletons and gills located under their shells. Reproduction in shrimp is sexual, but with an unusual twist. Most shrimp are protandric hermaphrodites, animals that begin life as males, then change into females during midlife. After fertilization, developing eggs cling to the female's swimming legs, where they remain until they hatch. Shrimp larvae swim freely for two or three months before settling into the mature shrimp lifestyle in the water column or on the seafloor.

There are many kinds of shrimp that live in continental shelf waters. Coonstripe (*Pandalus hypsinotus*), sidestripe (*Pandalus gurneyi*), pink (various species), and humpback (*Pandalus hypsinotus*) shrimp are just a few. Coonstripes, which have white and red stripes, reach lengths of 5.5 inches

Fig. 4.4   Some isopods are parasitic, like those living on this grouper. (Courtesy of the Sanctuary Collection, NOAA)

(14 cm), and are found in waters ranging from intertidal to depths of 606 feet (184.7 m). Sidestripe shrimp can tolerate waters as deep as 2,100 feet (640.1 m) and are more likely to be found over muddy bottoms. Their pale orange bodies display long stripes laterally and may grow to 8.2 inches (20.8 cm) in length. Crests, or humps, on their heads give the humpback shrimp their names. Their 7.5-inch (19.2-cm)-long bodies display white and red bands. Pink shrimp are smaller than humpbacks, usually averaging 6.9 inches (17.5 cm) long.

The northern or American lobster (*Homarus americanus*) can be found intertidally on rocky substrates to depths of 1,312 feet (400 m). Growing as long as three feet (90 cm), American lobsters have three pairs of legs and a pair of strong pinching claws. Adult lobsters use their claws to dig out living quarters under rocks. Some American lobsters travel, covering a range that extends 6.2 to 9.3 miles (10 to 15 km). When lobsters are alive, their color is brown or mottled green. When cooked, red pigment that is bound to protein in living organisms is freed, and it colors the animal's exoskeleton.

Squat lobsters (*Munidopsis*) closely resemble their American lobster relatives but live entirely different lifestyles. Squat lobsters do not have a hard exoskeleton covering their abdomens, so they must protect their soft body parts by backing into cracks and crevices between rocks, leaving only their claws exposed. Once tucked into a safe place, squat lobsters use their claws to keep away intruders and sift through nearby sand for edible material. These animals play important roles as scavengers in the continental shelf food webs.

Like shrimp and lobsters, crabs are crustaceans that have protective exoskeletons. The bodies of crabs are flattened, an adaptation that allows them to squeeze into small spaces between rocks where they are protected from waves and predators. Crabs mate in shallow waters near the shore, but females often travel to deeper waters to find appropriate spots to lay their eggs. Most crabs are active, aggressive animals that both scavenge and prey on small animals.

The Dungeness crab (*Cancer magister*), a brown or tan animal, is abundant over sandy bottoms and in beds of sea grass.

When the weather is cold or stormy, groups of female Dungeness crabs with fertilized eggs attached to their legs congregate in deep water, where they partially bury their bodies in the sediment. After eggs hatch, larval crabs undergo a series of molts and changes until they reach maturity, a period of about two years.

Scavenging bits of food as they go, spider crabs move very slowly over the seafloor on long, spindly legs. To avoid the notice of predators, the crabs camouflage themselves by hooking bits of algae to the sharp spines of their shells. The common spider crab (*Libinia emarginata*) can be found from sublittoral zones to water 400 feet (121.9 m) deep. Sexes are easily differentiated because males have legs and pincers that are almost twice as long as those of the females.

Porcelain crabs (*Petrolisthes*) are so named because their legs break off easily. For this species, losing a limb is a life-saving strategy. If snared by a predator, a porcelain crab can abandon its trapped leg and scurry away. Once a crab regains its freedom, lost body parts quickly regenerate. The bodies of these crabs are extremely flattened, and the pinching claws large.

A close relative of the porcelain crab is the hermit crab. Like squat lobsters, hermit crabs lack exoskeletons on their abdomens. To protect themselves, they back into snail shells and grasp them with their highly modified, hindmost legs. When they travel, hermit crabs drag the shells along with them.

Sea Spiders and Horseshoe Crabs

Two types of crablike animals, horseshoe crabs and sea spiders, are members of a primitive group of arthropods called chelicerates. All chelicerates lack antennae and jaws. Without jaws, they must eat prey that is liquefied or in extremely small particles. Many have a pair of pincerlike eating appendages called chelicerae. Terrestrial chelicerates include ticks, spiders, and scorpions.

Sea spiders differ from their terrestrial cousins in several ways. Unlike true spiders, whose bodies are made of two segments, sea spiders have three distinct body parts. In addition, sea spiders do not spin webs, and they have from four to six pairs of legs instead of four pairs. To feed, a sea spider pierces the body of a soft invertebrate, like an anemone, with its tubular proboscis, then sucks out the internal tissue. Most sea spiders are extremely small, measuring only one-sixteenth of an inch (two mm) in length. The female lays eggs, which are externally fertilized by the male, the smaller of the pair. After fertilization, the male glues the eggs to his legs to protect them until they hatch.

More than 600 species of sea spiders are found worldwide. Rare in tropical waters, the greatest number of species is found near Antarctica. Giant sea spiders, member of the genus *Colossendeis* that have leg spans as wide as 19.7 inches (50 cm), live in this cold region.

The shell of the Atlantic horseshoe crab (*Limulus polyphemus*) ends in a long tail that serves as a rudder as the animal swims. Two compound eyes and two simple eyes are situated on the dorsal side of the horseshoe-shaped shell. Underneath the shell are the mouth, five pairs of legs, and gills. Horseshoe crabs feed on burrowing mollusks and worms.

Horseshoe crabs mate and lay eggs in shallow, intertidal waters. During mating, the smaller male hangs onto the female's back, attaching himself with special hooks located on his first pair of legs. The female digs a hole and deposits her eggs, which are immediately fertilized by the male, then both adults return to deeper shelf waters.

Echinoderms

The floor of the continental shelf is dotted with echinoderms, a group of spiny-skinned animals that include starfish, sea cucumbers, sand dollars, and sea urchins. The spines protruding on an echinoderm's dorsal surface are part of its internal calcium carbonate skeleton. At the base of the spines, tiny pincers called pedicellariae work constantly to keep the body free of debris and parasites.

All echinoderms are radially symmetrical, and most have five or more arms extending from a central disk. The mouth of a starfish is located in the center of its body, on the ventral side, and the anus on the dorsal surface. Depending on the species, echinoderms can be carnivores, detritivores, or herbivores.

Echinoderms possess tube feet, shown in Figure 4.5, that act like suction cups, The suction cups are operated by a system of tubes that carry water. As the feet press against objects, water is withdrawn, creating suction. When water is returned to the cups, the suction is broken and the tube feet release their grip.

To reproduce, echinoderms release sperm and eggs that fuse in the water to form zygotes, then larvae. Larvae swim in the plankton before settling to the bottom and taking on typical adult echinoderm features. Most echinoderms can also reproduce asexually. If part of the animal breaks off, it may grow into a complete, new organism. All are capable of regenerating missing body parts, including limbs, spines, and in some cases, intestines.

Starfish are echinoderms that have five to 40 arms radiating from a central disk. Many are predators who will eat any small

Fig. 4.5   On its ventral side, a starfish has a centrally located mouth surrounded by five arms that are covered in tube feet. The anus is located on the dorsal side; the skin on the dorsal side is covered with spines. (Courtesy of Dr. James P. McVey, NOAA Sea Grant Program)

fish or invertebrate they can catch. Some foods are more difficult to get at than others, but sea stars are up to the challenge. To feed on the soft body of a tightly closed mussel, a starfish uses its tube feet to pull apart the shells. Instead of drawing the food into its mouth, the starfish does just the opposite; it pushes its stomach through the opening between the shells. Digestive juices in the starfish's stomach dissolve the mussel tissue, which the stomach then absorbs. When the meal is over, the starfish pulls its stomach back in place and crawls to another mussel.

Starfish occur in all shapes and sizes. The huge, many-rayed or sunflower star (*Pycnopodia helianthoides*) grows to about five feet (1.5 m) in diameter. The sunflower star is the fastest echinoderm, capable of traveling across the bottom at rates up to 40 inches (101.6 cm) per minute. A smaller species, the crown-of-thorns star (*Acanthaster planci*) preys on corals. The dorsal side of this red sea star is covered in sharp, slightly venomous spines. The most abundant sea star on the west coast of the United States is the bat star (*Asterina miniata*). Occurring in purple, orange, or red, bat stars have short arms and measure only four inches (10.2 cm) in diameter. They are common sights on rocky and sandy bottoms, as well as in sea grass and kelp beds.

Found at all depths of the ocean, brittle stars are small, thin echinoderms that use their flexible arms for swimming. Brittle stars get their names from the ease with which their arms break off if caught by a predator. Like all echinoderms, brittle stars are able to regenerate lost body parts, and regrow the damaged arm in a short time. They feed on detritus and microscopic organisms on the seafloor.

There are more species of brittle stars than any other echinoderm. Schayer's brittle star (*Ophionereis schayeri*) is the largest species in Australian waters. Its gray and white striped arms are long, giving the echinoderm a diameter of 11.8 inches (30 cm). The daisy brittle star (*Ophiopholis aculeate*), about 21 inches (53.3 cm) wide, can be red, orange, yellow, purple, blue, tan, or black. Rocks and the holdfasts of kelps provide hiding places where the daisy brittle star spends most of its time resting, although the animal can move quickly if threatened.

▲ *Tall kelp plants form unique habitats on the continental shelf.*
(Courtesy of NOAA)

▲ *Sea grass helps hold soil in place and provides food and homes for sea animals on the continental shelf.* (Courtesy of Paige Grill, NOAA)

▲ *The mouth of an anemone is surrounded by stinging tentacles.*
(Courtesy of Kathy Castro, NOAA)

▲ *The purple-striped jellyfish lives in the relatively shallow waters of the continental shelf.* (Courtesy of Kip Evans, NOAA)

▲ *Krill are small crustaceans that live in the cold waters of the Southern Ocean.* (Courtesy of Jamie Hall, NOAA)

▲ *Orange colonies of tunicates grow on surfaces such as shells, rocks, and the pilings of piers.* (Courtesy of NOAA, Sanctuary Collection)

▲ *Barracuda are large fish with razor-sharp teeth.* (Courtesy of NOAA)

◀ *The seahorse wraps its tail around algae to maintain its position in the water.* (Courtesy of Mr. Mohammed Al Momany, Aqaba, Jordan, NOAA)

▲ *White sharks are formidable predators in the waters of the continental shelf.* (Courtesy of Scott Anderson, NOAA)

▲ *Sea snakes are marine reptiles that never leave the ocean.*
(Courtesy of NOAA)

◀ *The emperor penguin is the largest of the penguin species.* (Courtesy of Michael Van Woert, NOAA, NESDIS, ORA)

◀ *Horned puffins, with their boldly marked black and white bodies and bright orange legs and beaks, share a rocky outcrop with red-breasted cormorants.* (Courtesy of Captain Budd Christman, NOAA)

▲ *Blue-footed boobies are seabirds that have stout bodies and thick beaks.* (Courtesy of Rosalind Cohen, NODC, NOAA)

▲ *A sea otter floats on its back and dines on a sea urchin.* (Courtesy of NOAA)

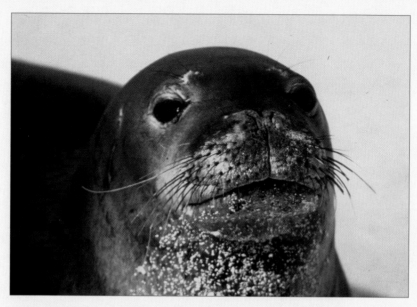

▲ *The Hawaiian monk seal spends its time ashore resting on the beach.* (Courtesy of U.S. Fish and Wildlife Service)

▲ *In continental shelf waters, dolphins often swim and jump alongside boats.* (Courtesy of NOAA)

Recent research on the brittle star *Ophiocoma wendtii* has shed light on the way echinoderms gain information about their environment. Scientists have found that the top side of *Ophiocoma wendtii*'s body is covered with tiny, light-sensitive lens. These multiple lenses might work together like a compound eye to help the brittle star get out of the way of predators or find food. The discovery of lenses in *Ophiocoma* leads scientists to speculate that other echinoderms might have similar light-sensitive structures.

Sea urchins are round invertebrates whose bodies are covered in long spines. Like other echinoderms, their tissues are supported by a rigid internal skeleton. The mouth of a sea urchin is a unique arrangement of five teeth that forms a beaklike chewing structure called Aristotle's lantern. Favorite foods of sea urchins include kelp and other seaweeds.

The body of a purple sea urchin (*Arbacia punctulata*) is covered in one-inch (2.5-cm) purple spines. Found on rocky bottoms, or among seaweeds, purple sea urchins live from the intertidal zone to water that is 750 feet (229 m) deep. As omnivores, the animals eat dead or dying plant and animal matter, algae, sponges, corals, and clams.

Red sea urchins (*Strongylocentrotus franciscanus*) live in the shallow waters of the Pacific Ocean, where they feed on algae and grow to be 5.9 inches (15 cm) in diameter. Research conducted by the Oregon State University (OSU) and the Lawrence Livermore National Laboratory shows that red sea urchins are long-lived animals that commonly survive 100 years, and may even live to be 200 years old. According to Thomas Ebert, a marine zoologist at OSU, urchins do not show signs as aging from year to year like other kinds of animals. Most of the sea urchins studied so far did not die of old age but from disease or predation. Ebert and other scientists are interested in finding out why the urchins do not age.

Although sea urchins and sea cucumbers are close relatives, their bodies have very different shapes. A sea cucumber is longer from mouth to anus than any other kind of echinoderm, giving it the appearance of a fat worm. Instead of lying on its mouth like a sea star, a sea cucumber reclines on its side. To move, the animal contracts the muscles in its leathery body, or crawls slowly on ventral tube feet. Around a sea cucumber's mouth, several tube feet are modified to form tentacles. In some species tentacles strain suspended matter from the water, but others use them to shovel sand into their mouths so they can digest the organic matter in it. If a sea cucumber is threatened, it may eject tubules or bits of its intestines on an intruder. The sticky, spaghetti-like entrails confuse the intruder and give the sea cucumber a chance to escape. Like other echinoderms, the sea cucumber can regenerate its lost body parts.

Sea cucumbers are found at all depths of the continental shelf waters. The California sea cucumber (*Parastichopus californicus*) can be dark red or brown, and grows up to 16 inches (40 cm) long. The orange-colored burrowing sea cucumber (*Cucumaria miniata*), a 10-inch (25-cm) long species, hides in shallow-water sea grass beds. The warty sea cucumber (*Parastichopus parvimensis*) is named for the numerous black projections on its skin.

Tunicates

Tunicates are small animals with rounded shapes that are found through the seas. Commonly known as sea squirts, tunicates are named for the tough, cellulose-like tunics that cover their bodies. Depending on the species, they may be solitary or colonial, like the orange species shown in the lower color insert on page C-3.

Many species have a tadpole-like larval stage that exhibits many of the characteristics of higher organisms, including a nerve cord. An adult tunicate has two siphons, one incurrent and one excurrent, that circulate water through its body. Benthic species spend their adult lives attached to one place, but open-water tunicates have tails that enable them to swim. A special gland produces mucus that is used to form a net or house that collects food particles. When a tunicate's house becomes clogged, it is discarded and a new one woven. Old houses are important sources of food for many zooplankton.

One group of tunicates, the salps, is made up of small, swimming organisms that congregate in shelf waters by the millions. Each animal's body is enclosed in a see-through covering or test. By pumping water through the test, an organism swims forward in the water. Water streaming through the test also brings in suspended food material, which the salps extract.

Conclusion

Mollusks, crustaceans, and echinoderms are three major groups of complex invertebrates found in waters of the continental shelf. The bodies of these animals show many evolutionary advances over those of sponges, cnidarians, and worms.

The majority of mollusks have soft bodies, rough tongue-like radulae, and some form of shell. Mollusks found in shelf waters include gastropods, bivalves, and cephalopods. Snails, limpets, whelks, conchs, and nudibranchs are classified as gastropods, animals characterized by a "stomach foot," because their locomotive structure is located near the center of their bodies. The shells of snails, whelks, and conchs are spiraled, while those of limpets are not. Nudibranchs, which lack shells, resemble large flatworms. As protection, many nudibranchs produce toxins.

The soft bodies of bivalves are protected by two tough shells that are held together by a hinge. Clams, scallops, and mussels are typical continental shelf bivalves. Clams have a centrally located, muscular foot that they use for burrowing, crawling, or swimming, but scallops and mussels lack a foot. Instead, they live on the top of the sediment and move by squirting water through their siphons. The foot of a cephalopod is modified as a ring of tentacles located near the head. Tentacles can be used for movement or to grab prey. Cephalopods have nervous systems that are more advanced than those of any other invertebrates, and they show the ability to learn.

Two groups of arthropods are found on the continental shelf: crustaceans and chelicerates. The bodies of all arthropods are covered with tough exoskeletons and have jointed appendages. Exoskeletons protect arthropods from predators. To grow, an arthropod must shed this bulky covering, a practice that makes it vulnerable. Most crustaceans mate after the female of the species has just shed her exoskeleton.

Crustaceans include such well-known sea creatures as shrimp, crabs, and lobsters. All have segmented bodies and antennae as well as feeding, walking, and swimming appendages. Isopods, amphipods, krill, and shrimp are small crustaceans; crabs and lobster are larger. The American lobster can reach lengths of up to three feet (0.9 m) long in the waters off both the East and West Coasts of the United States, although most are smaller.

More closely related to spiders than crabs, the horseshoe crab and sea spider are classified as chelicerates. Both have mouth parts that are used for piercing and sucking juices. Only one species of horseshoe crab exists, *Limulus polyphemus*. On the other hand, sea spiders are represented by more than 600 species, with the greatest diversity in Antarctic waters.

The spiny-skinned animals, or echinoderms, include starfish, sea urchins, sand dollars, and sea cucumbers. Unique to this group is a water vascular system that powers suction cup–like tube feet for movement and grasping. Echinoderms also share incredible powers of regeneration, and can regrow lost limbs and internal organs.

Many starfish are carnivores that prey on bivalves, opening the shells of prey with their tube feet and inverting their ventrally located stomachs inside. Sea urchins are globe-shaped animals with long spines, some of which are poisonous. Most graze on kelp and other macroalgae. Sea cucumbers are elongated, with tube feet modified as tentacles around the mouth that enable them to vacuum up the food-rich sediments.

5

Fish
The Most Successful Continental Shelf Vertebrates

Fish in continental shelf waters form living mosaics, swimming vertically, diagonally, and horizontally through a three-dimensional world. The routines of many nearshore fish take them along extensive paths that lead to the seacoast or out into the open ocean. Others are so highly specialized that they spend their entire lives within a very small zone of the sea.

Fish are the largest group of vertebrates in the world. The particular mix of fish species found in any area of the shelf depends on the blend of factors such as nutrients, substrates, water currents, temperature, salinity, water depth, and light that exist in that region. The amount of light that can penetrate the water, and the depth of its penetration, affects several other qualities of the habitat. In shallow, nutrient-rich water, light makes its way into the entire water column and supports ample populations of phytoplankton, food for many kinds of small fish. As water deepens, light intensity diminishes and so do the levels of phytoplankton. In deep regions where food resources are low, fewer kinds, and smaller populations, of fish are found.

The shallow waters of the continental shelf are excellent homes for juveniles of many fish species. Macroalgae and sea grass are much more abundant in shallow water than in deep. These plants provide young fish with food and hiding places from predators, giving them opportunities to eat and grow before facing life in the more barren and dangerous open seas.

Fish living in continental shelf waters show tremendous variation. Some fish spend their time swimming in groups, many swim alone, and others lie on the seafloor. Fish with similar physical traits are classified in large groups called families. Many of the species in one family show the same types of lifestyle.

Schooling

Fish often school, or swim together, in large groups. Schools of fish may be polarized, with all the fish swimming in the same direction, or non-polarized, with fish swimming in many directions. Both types of schools improve an individual fish's chance of survival. A large school of fish may be able to confuse a predator into thinking that it is one big, dangerous organism instead of a group of small, helpless fish. In addition, if a fish is in a school, it stands a good chance of being spared when a predator does attack. Plus, a school of fish has more lookouts than one fish swimming alone, and is more likely to notice danger.

Some kinds of fish, such as groupers, only form schools when it is time to *spawn*. This strategy ensures that the males and females will release their gametes into the water at the same time. If egg predators are nearby, they will eat some of the eggs but may not be able to eat all of them, so some will probably survive. Foraging for food can also bring a group of fish together. As a school, foraging fish like mackerel and herring have plenty of sets of eyes that improve the chances of finding something to eat. By working as a team, the school may be able to overwhelm and take prey that one fish alone could not handle.

Schooling Fish

Fish that live around the continental shelf, but stay in the upper layer of water, generally have streamlined bodies and are very adept at swimming. Many of these fish congregate in groups called *schools*. The formation of schools is evident in plankton-eaters such as herring and anchovies as well as in predatory fish like tuna and mackerel. Fish are able to maintain their positions in schools using their *lateral lines* and senses, such as sight, touch, and smell.

Two species of schooling fish are tuna and mackerel, both members of the family Scombridae. These powerful, swift swimmers occasionally leave the shelf to venture out to the open sea. Tuna and mackerel can be found in cold temperate climates as well as in the tropics, where they are preyed on by sharks and toothed whales.

The little tunny (*Euthynnus alletteratus*), also known as the mackerel tuna or the Atlantic little tuna, is found worldwide in neritic waters. These robust, torpedo-shaped fish are steel blue in color, averaging 32 inches (81 cm) in length and weighing about 20 pounds (9.1 kg). Little tunny are opportunistic predators that will eat anything available, but prefer crustaceans, squid, herring, and sardines. Their close relatives, the Atlantic mackerel (*Scomber scombrus*), travel in schools that can exceed 1,000 fish. In a mackerel school, all the fish are about the same size, an arrangement that enables the school to maintain a constant speed. These swift swimmers, found on both sides of the Atlantic Ocean, prey on herring, squid, and shrimp. During the winter, Atlantic mackerel stay in deep water, but in the spring they migrate toward the shore. Spawning takes place near the surface, and eggs are allowed to float in the water column as they develop.

A favorite prey of tuna and mackerel are members of the herring family, Clupeidae. Herring are schooling fish that feed on zooplankton. One representative of Clupeidae, the Atlantic menhaden (*Brevoortia tyrannus*), is silver with dark shoulder spots, a forked caudal fin, and spineless fins. Ranging from Nova Scotia to Florida, these animals spawn in waters over the continental shelf. The free swimming larvae spend some time over the continental shelf before going to bays and estuaries to mature. They remain in estuarine environments until it is time to return to the sea as adults to feed on phytoplankton, organic detritus, and zooplankton. Schools of menhaden are preyed on by bluefish, mackerel, tuna, sharks, herons, egrets, osprey, or eagles. Atlantic menhaden, nicknamed "bugmouth fish," usually have a large crustacean parasite living on or near their mouths.

A carnivorous fish that demonstrates schooling behavior and migrates to the inshore regions of the continental shelves is the bluefish (*Pomatomus saltatrix*). A member of the Pomatomidae family, the bluefish gets its name from the blue-green coloration on its dorsal side. Bluefish have large heads, low first dorsal fins, and mouths that are extended behind the eyes. Their mouths are large and gaping, and filled with prominent, razor-sharp teeth. Adult fish of about equal size travel in schools together, preying on fish, squid, and eels. Located from Nova Scotia to Argentina, bluefish schools work as teams to drive smaller schools of fish toward shallow water. Once the small fish are cornered, the bluefish move in, kill them, and feed. During this feast, the fierce predators eat until they are so full that they regurgitate, then go back to eating until all the food is gone.

A predatory fish that both schools and swims alone is the barracuda, in the upper color insert on page C-4, a member of family Sphyraenidae. The largest species of this family is the great barracuda (*Sphyraena barracuda*), a greenish fish with dark bars on its sides. An adult great barracuda is an ominous sight, with a slender body that is four to six feet (1.2 to 1.8 m) long, large sharp teeth that protrude from its mouth, powerful jaws, a serrated dorsal fin, and a forked tail. These predators can be found worldwide, but they have a special preference for warm seas. Adults range from the open ocean to the inshore waters, where they often congregate in sea grass beds. Great barracuda may be seen in the western Atlantic Ocean, from Massachusetts to Brazil, from the Gulf of Mexico to the Caribbean Sea, in the eastern Atlantic Ocean, and Indo-Pacific Ocean.

The favorite prey of barracuda are mullet, anchovy, and grunts, but the big fish have been known to attack humans on rare occasions. In most cases, human attacks have occurred when waders or swimmers enter the water wearing colorful clothing or carrying shiny objects that the fish mistake for prey.

Groundfish

Not all schooling fish spend their time near the surface of the water; some can be found on or near the bottom on the continental shelf. These bottom dwellers are known as demersal or groundfish. The family Gadidae is made up of demersal schooling fish, including the Atlantic cod (*Gadus morhua*), a specimen that has a heavy body, three dorsal fins, and two anal fins. The Atlantic cod's head is large and distinguished by a protruding lower jaw and fleshy barbels that stick out like whiskers.

Although primarily found within a few feet of the ocean floor, the Atlantic cod will travel between deep and shallow waters over most of the Atlantic Ocean during spawning season and when in search of food. These fish have the ability to change colors to match their surroundings and may appear in shades of green, gray, red, or brown, dotted with small dark spots over their bodies. Their diets are variable and include plankton, worms, mollusks, crustaceans, and other fish. Atlantic cod range in weight from six to 12 pounds (2.7 to 5.4 kg) and are preyed upon by sharks and pollock.

Colorization

One of the most striking features of fish is their colorization. Coloring and body marks on fish help them avoid predators by staying out of sight. Many prey species, such as gulf flounder, avoid being eaten by blending in with their surroundings, matching the subtle shades of their habitats. Spotted fish look like the seafloor, and striped fish blend in with grasses. Some reef fish display bright colors because they live among brightly colored sponges and corals.

Conversely, coloring that mimics fish's habitats helps predators get close to their prey. The ability to avoid detection is a significant advantage for such hunters as scorpion fish that wait quietly until prey comes within striking distance. A hunter is able to conserve both time and energy if it does not have to pursue its food.

Most fish, including sea trout and grouper, display some degree of countershading. This form of coloring reduces the clarity of the fish's body outline in water. The simplest, and most common, form of countershading is a dark dorsal side and a pale ventral side, with intermediate colors between the two. When sunlight filters down through the water, it lightens the fish's back and throws shadows on its underside. The overall effect of countershading lessens the degree of contrast between the fish and the water.

A few species of fish, such as the spotfin butterfly fish and the high hat fish, show disruptive or deflective colorization that includes bands, stripes, or dots of contrasting colors. These colors and patterns confuse predators by distorting the true shape, size, and position of the fish. Bright patterns draw the predator's eye, causing it to see the pattern rather than the fish itself. This type of coloring can deflect the predator's attention away from a fish's vulnerable areas, such as its head and eyes.

Colorization can also be used as an advertisement. There is no point in being poisonous and unpalatable if no one knows it. Instead of hiding, poisonous fish announce their dangerous status. Fish may also advertise their age or sex with coloring. Males are generally more colorful than females, whose duller shades help camouflage and protect them. Young fish may be transparent or pale, making it hard for predators to spot them, as well as letting the older fish of their own species know that they are not a threat.

Haddock (*Melanogrammus aeglefinus*) and pollock (*Pollachius virens*) are two other members of family Gadidae. A haddock, which may weigh from five to 10 pounds (2.3 to 4.5 kg), is dark gray on top and silver gray underneath, with a distinguishing black, thumbprintlike spot located above each pectoral fin. These fish school in open water and prefer areas along the American and European coasts of the Atlantic Ocean, where the seafloor is covered in smooth rock or sand. Pollock, which range in size from four to 15 pounds (1.8 to 6.8 kg), have similar body shapes but possess snouts that are pointed and lower jaws that protrude. After over-wintering offshore in the Atlantic Ocean, large schools of pollock move inshore in the spring and congregate over rocky bottoms off the American and European coasts.

Rocky substrates also attract groundfish of the family Cyclopteridae, a group commonly known as lumpsuckers or lumpfish. Instead of scales, the bodies of these unusual fish are covered with bony plates. Each fish is equipped with a sucker disc on its ventral surface that is used to attach the fish to hard substrates, such as rocks. *Cyclopterus lumpus* is a lumpsucker that measures about 16 inches (40.6 cm) in length and has a tiny mouth. This fish comes inshore to spawn in the summer, but during the rest of the year it can be found in colder waters of continental shelves.

Also lurking among rocky substrates are fish that belong to family Syngnathidae. Atypical in shape, members of this family have bodies that are long and covered with bony rings rather than scales. These fish have small, toothless mouths that are located at the ends of their snouts, and they lack pelvic fins. Males in this family possess a brood pouch in which the eggs are cared for until they hatch.

The pipefish (*Sygnathus facus*), a member of the Syngnathidae family, can be found from depths of five to 366 feet (1.5 to 111.6 m) in waters that range from Canada to Florida and through the Gulf of Mexico. Pipefish measure about 15.8 inches (40 cm) in length and spend part of their lives in estuaries. Adult fish eat crustaceans, fish eggs, and the young of other fish species. Seahorses (*Hippocampus*), shown in the lower color insert on page C-4, are also members of this family. Because they are very poor swimmers, seahorses have to conceal themselves from predators to avoid being eaten. A seahorse has brownish coloration and a head that is perpendicular to its vertical body. Found worldwide, most of these fish prefer to live among eelgrass and sargassum weed, where they are camouflaged from predators and can lie in wait for their own prey.

Bottom Dwellers

Although ground fish of the continental shelf live close to the seafloor, another group of fish lives below them. Flatfish lie on their sides on the substrate with both eyes facing upward. Abundant in warm, shallow water around the world, flatfish belong to the families Bothidae (left-eyed flounder or turbots), Pleuronectidae (right-eyed flounder), and Soleidae (sole). The bodies of these fish are not actually flat but seem to be so because they swim on their sides. Their lengths can range from a few inches up to several feet.

From a physiological point of view, one of the most interesting events in the life of any flatfish occurs in the juvenile stage. A hatchling has one eye located on each side of its heads, like other species of fish. As the young fish matures, the bones of the skull and mouth undergo a transformation that causes one eye to migrate to either the left or right side of its head, depending on the species' genetic code. By adulthood, when the fish travels to the bottom of the continental shelf, both eyes are on one side of the head. A mature flatfish spends the majority of its time resting on the sandy ocean bottom. It can change color to blend in with the surroundings, an adaptation that helps the fish avoid predators. The only clue to its presence is a pair of protruding eyes that constantly scan the waters overhead in search of predators or prey. If pursued or disturbed, a flatfish quickly swims away by using a fluttering motion that throws up a silt screen around its body. Once the fish is safely out of harm's way, it settles back down on its side. Most flatfish eat whatever creatures they can find on the bottom environment, including invertebrates and small fish.

Turbots (*Psetta maxima*), or left-eyed flounders, have both eyes on the left side of their heads. Turbots are circular in shape and the left sides of their bodies are dark-colored and marked with large bony knots. These scale-less fish can grow up to 3.3 feet (1 m) in length and are as broad as they are tall. Atlantic halibuts (*Hippoglossus hippoglossus*), also known as right-eyed flounders, live in waters on both sides of the Atlantic Ocean. They are among the largest flatfish and can be distinguished from similar species by their distinctive big mouths and forked tails. Closely related are plaice (*Pleuronectes platessa*), which are greenish-olive fish that have orange spots.

Another group of bottom dwellers found on the continental shelf are the anglerfish of the family Ogcocephalidae. The dorsal fins of Ogcocephalidae are modified as long spines with fleshy tips that dangle over the fishes' mouths like living lures. When an unsuspecting passerby investigates a lure, the anglerfish lunges forward and grabs it. One angler, the polka dot batfish (*Ogcocephalus radiatus*), is unusual because it is a poor swimmer. A batfish's pectoral and pelvic fins are modified for walking on the bottom of the ocean. The bodies of these peculiar-looking fish are tan to orange in color, with dark spots trimmed in white, and their fins are trimmed in orange. The mouths of batfish jut into a sharp downward point, and the caudal fins are tiny and round. These bottom-dwelling organisms, found in many parts of the Atlantic Ocean, cover themselves in mud or sand so they can ambush worms and small crustaceans.

Skates and rays also live near the floor of the continental shelf. Many spend their time burrowed in mud or sand with only their eyes protruding. These fish can survive in a burrowed position because they breathe through two *spiracles* located near their eyes on top of their body. Skates, members of family Rajidae, are adapted to both nearshore and deep sea habitats. One type of skate found on the continental shelf is the big skate (*Raja binoculata*), named because it can grow to eight feet (2.4 m) in length. Huge black circles on its fins look very much like eyes and help to scare away predators. The big skate's body is a grayish color that blends in perfectly with the ocean floor, protecting it from any sharks that might be patrolling the area. The big skate can be found in nearshore waters along the western coast of North America. On the other extreme, the little skate (*Raja erinacea*) grows to only

21 inches (53 cm) long. These small skates are found in shallow waters over sand and gravel from the Gulf of St. Lawrence to the North Carolina coast.

Rays and skates are very similar but differ in the shapes of their pelvic fins: Those of skates are convex on the outer edge, while the rays' pelvic fins are concave. Whiptail stingrays, members of family Dasyatidae, are characterized by sawlike, venomous spines. One whip-tail ray, *Dasyatis,* has a long tail studded with stiff venomous spines that can be used to impale enemies. These rays are potentially dangerous to unsuspecting swimmers and waders that may step on them. The Southern stingray (*Dasyatis americana*) has a rhombic shape with rounded outer corners. The top of this ray lacks a dorsal fin and is colored brown or gray, while the underside is white or light gray. Southern stingrays, found from New Jersey to Brazil, stay relatively close to shores and in bays, where they lie partially buried in sand with only the tail, eyes, and spiracles exposed.

The family Myliobatidae, a group known as the graceful rays, includes the eagle rays, which live in tropical waters. Eagle rays are extremely active, at times leaping out of the water and turning somersaults. The purpose of these leaps and flips is not known for sure, but they may be techniques to remove parasites or they could be displays of eagle ray play. The massive jaws and extendible snouts of these rays help them root out benthic invertebrates from the bottom of the ocean.

Sharks are closely related to rays and skates because they have similar cartilaginous skeletons. There are many families of sharks that spend time between the continental shelf and the open ocean. One of the most feared is the white shark (*Carcharodon carcharias*), featured in the upper color insert on page C-5, a member of family Lamnidae. Living at the top of its food chain, this blue-gray shark has very few predators. Primarily a resident of temperate regions, the white shark is occasionally spotted in tropical waters and subarctic zones. The great white shark is the only species that elevates its head above the surface of the water and will even jump completely out of the water when in pursuit of a seal or sea lion. Growing up to 21.5 feet (6.5 m) in length, this fish has a varied diet that

Shark Anatomy

Although there are many kinds of sharks, they all are similar anatomically. A shark's digestive system begins at the mouth, which is filled with teeth. Shark teeth are continuously produced, and at any time a shark may have 3,000 teeth arranged in six to 20 rows. As older teeth are lost from the front rows, younger ones move forward and replace them. Teeth are adapted to specific kinds of food. Depending on their species, sharks may have thin, daggerlike teeth for holding prey; serrated, wedge-shaped teeth for cutting and tearing; or small, conical teeth that can crush animals in shells.

The internal skeletons of sharks are made of cartilage, a lightweight and flexible bonelike material. Their external surfaces are very tough and rugged. Sharks have extremely flexible skin that is covered with placoid scales, each of which is pointed and has a rough edge on it. Shark fins are rigid and cannot be folded down like the fins of bony fish.

Like other aquatic organisms, sharks get the oxygen they need to live from the water. Compared to air, water contains a small percentage of dissolved oxygen. Surface waters may contain five milliliters of oxygen per liter of water, dramatically less than the 210 ml of oxygen per liter of air that is available to land animals. To survive, fish must be very efficient at removing and concentrating the oxygen in water.

In aquatic organisms, gills carry out the function of lungs in terrestrial animals. To respire, sharks pull water in through their mouths and *spiracles,* holes on top of their

includes other sharks, stingrays, turtles, mollusks, crustaceans, sea birds, seals, sea lions, dolphins, and porpoises.

Sharks of the family Triakidae spend their time near the ocean bottom in a relatively narrow zone that extends from Oregon to the Gulf of California in Mexico. One member of this family, the leopard shark (*Triakis semifasciata*), also called the cat shark, prefers areas of the continental shelf that are thick with kelp forests. When hunting in shallow water, leopard sharks use electroreceptors, cells that are sensitive to the electric energy produced by living things, to pinpoint prey buried in the mud. Some of their favorite foods are clams and worms, although leopard sharks also dine on smaller fish and crustaceans. In the juvenile stages, the bodies of these young sharks are covered with spots that provide camouflage in the heads. The water passes over their gills and exits through the gill slits on the sides of the head. Most species of sharks can pump water over their gills by opening and closing their mouths. Some sharks, the "ram ventilators," must swim continuously to move water over their gills. Oxygen in water is picked up by tiny blood vessels in the gills, then carried to the heart, a small two-chambered, S-shaped tube. From there, oxygenated blood is pumped to the rest of the body.

Sharks fertilize their eggs internally. Males transfer sperm to females using modified pelvic fins. Some species are *oviparous*, which means the female lays fertilized eggs. Shark eggs may be deposited in lagoons or shallow reef water, where they incubate for six to 15 months. Many of the eggs' cases are equipped with hairy or leathery tendrils that help hold them to rocks or plants. Other species are *viviparous*, so the embryos develop inside the mother and are born alive. Several species are *ovoviviparous*, which means that the embryo develops inside an egg within the female's body. The egg hatches inside the mother, the hatchling eats the yolk and any unfertilized eggs, then is born alive.

Shark populations are relatively small compared to other kinds of fish. One reason is because shark reproduction rates are low. Unlike fish and many of the invertebrates, a female shark produces only a few offspring each year. In addition, the gestation period, time when the embryo develops inside the mother, of viviparous species is long.

shallow waters. By maturity, the spots disappear and the 6.5-foot (two-m)-long sharks move into deeper water.

Sharks in the family Heterodontidae are not long and streamlined like most other types of sharks. One representative, the horn shark (*Heterodontus francisci*), has a flat, lumpy body that grows to lengths of four feet (1.2 m). Horn-shaped spines located in front of each dorsal fin account for the animal's common name. Hiding during the day in caves and under ledges in shelf waters of the eastern Pacific Ocean, this brownish green shark emerges at night to hunt small fish, mollusks, sea urchins, and crustaceans on the seafloor. Compared with other sharks, the horn shark is a poor swimmer and generally maneuvers about by crawling along the rocks with the help of its pectoral fins.

The requiem sharks, family Carcharhinidae, have streamlined bodies, rounded snouts, and sharp teeth. Unlike other families of sharks, these bottom swimmers possess a third eyelid that comes up from the bottom of their eyes when feeding and during conflict. One member of this family, the sandbar shark (*Carcharhinus plumbeus*), is both a predator and a scavenger of the ocean bottom. This brown shark, which can be seven feet (2.2 m) in length, lives in warm seas over muddy or sandy bottoms from the sublittoral zone to the outer edge of the continental shelf. Favorite foods include small bottom-dwelling fish, crustaceans, and mollusks. Sandbar sharks undergo extensive migrations, traveling from the seas near Cape Cod, their summer home, to more southern locations as the weather cools.

Found from the bottom to the surface, the dogfish sharks, family Squalidae, live on the continental shelf and out in the deep ocean. Dogfish sharks, like the one shown in Figure 5.1, have short snouts, two dorsal fins, no anal fins, and five gill slits. One species, the Cuban dogfish (*Squalus cubensis*), prefers warm, tropical waters around the outer continental shelf. Attaining lengths up to 43.3 inches (110 cm), although usually smaller, these gray animals have long spines on their dorsal fins, a concave edge on their pectoral fins, and no anal fin. To some people, dogfish sharks look dangerous, but their diets consist of small fish, mussels, and crustaceans. Even though they are not aggressive toward humans, contact with the spines on their dorsal fins can cause painful stings.

Not all sharks are carnivores. Members of family Cetorhinidae are plankton-eaters. The basking shark (*Cetorhinus maximus*) is the second-largest fish in the world, exceeded in size only by the whale shark (*Rhincodon typus*), another plankton-eater. Weighing more than four tons and measuring up to 29.5 feet (9 m) in length, this gray-brown giant has tiny teeth and a mouth that extends well behind the eyes. Also known as sun fish, basking sharks swim in shallow surface waters of temperate zones in the summer, migrating to deeper waters in the winter. Unaggressive animals, they feed by swimming with their mouths gaping wide so they can filter plankton from the water.

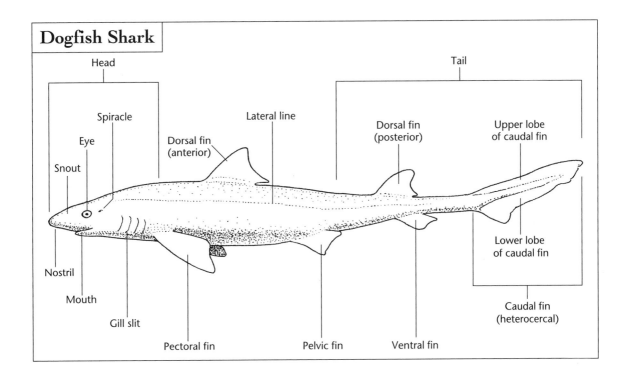

Dogfish Shark

Head — Tail

Spiracle — Lateral line — Dorsal fin (posterior) — Upper lobe of caudal fin

Eye — Dorsal fin (anterior)

Snout

Lower lobe of caudal fin

Nostril

Mouth

Caudal fin (heterocercal)

Gill slit

Pectoral fin — Pelvic fin — Ventral fin

Fish of Rocky Reefs and Kelp Beds

Groves of giant kelp resemble underwater forests and serve as homes for many species of fish. Like terrestrial forests, kelp forests provide a variety of places for animals to live and feed. Some fish spend their entire lives in kelp forests, defending their feeding zones with displays of *territorial behavior*. Others travel through the kelp looking for food wherever it is available. Darting among the kelps and the rocks on which they grow, rockfishes, family Sebastidae, and cabezons, family Cottidae, are two types of fish frequently found in kelp beds. The rosy rockfish (*Sebastes rosaceus*), which is red with purple spots, is also known as a rock cod or a Pacific red snapper. Living along the Pacific coast from California to Washington State, rosy rockfish reach lengths of nearly one foot (30.5 cm). They prey on smaller fish, shrimp, and octopuses that live among the rocks. Blue rockfish (*Sebastes mystinus*) have dorsal and anal fins that contain mildly venomous spines.

Fig. 5.1   Typical shark external anatomy is displayed by the dogfish shark. Special sensory structures include the lateral line and the ampullae of Lorenzini, located inside the snout.

Bony Fish Anatomy

All bony fish share many physical characteristics, which are labeled in Figure 5.2. One of their distinguishing features is scaly skin. Scales on fish overlap one another, much like shingles on a roof, protecting the skin from damage and slowing the movement of water into or out of the fish's body.

Bony fish are outfitted with fins that facilitate maneuvering and positioning in the water. The fins, which are made of thin membranes supported by stiff pieces of cartilage, can be folded down or held upright. Fins are named for their location: Dorsal fins are on the back, a caudal fin is at the tail, and an anal fin is on the ventral side. Two sets of lateral fins are located on the sides of the fish, the pectoral fins are toward the head, and the pelvic fins are near the tail. The caudal fin moves the fish forward in the water, and the others help change direction and maintain balance.

Although fish dine on a wide assortment of food, most species are predators whose mouths contain small teeth for grasping prey. Nutrients from digested food are distributed through the body by a system of closed blood vessels. The circulation of blood is powered by a muscular two-chambered heart. Blood entering the heart is depleted of oxygen and filled with carbon dioxide, a waste product of metabolism. Blood collects in the upper chamber, the atrium, before it is pushed into the ventricle. From the ventricle, it travels to the gills where it picks up oxygen and gets rid of its carbon dioxide. Water exits through a single gill slit on the side of the head. The gill slits of fish are covered with a protective flap, the operculum.

In many bony fish, some gases in the blood are channeled into another organ, the swim bladder. This organ is essentially a gas bag that helps the fish control its depth by adjusting its buoyancy. A fish can float higher in the water by increasing the volume of gas in the swim bladder. To sink, the fish reduces the amount of gas in the bladder.

Most bony fish reproduce externally. Females lay hundreds of eggs in the water, then males swim by and release milt, a fluid containing sperm, on the eggs. Fertilization occurs in the open water, and the parents swim away, leaving the eggs unprotected. Not all of the eggs are fertilized, and many that are fertilized will become victims of predators, so only a small percentage of eggs hatch.

Fig. 5.2   The special features of bony fish include bony scales (a), opercula (b), highly maneuverable fins (c), a tail with its upper and lower lobes usually of equal size (d), a swim bladder that adjusts the fish's buoyancy (e), nostrils (f), pectoral fins (g), a pelvic fin (h), an anal fin (i), lateral lines (j), dorsal fins (k), and a stomach (l).

Features of Bony Fish

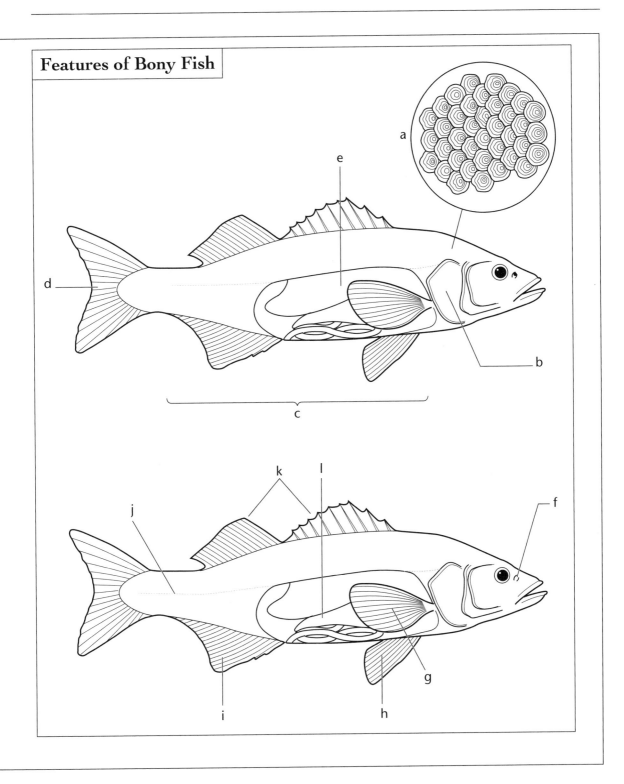

These fish prefer to swim near the rocky bottoms and may stay in waters as deep as 18,000 feet (5,486.4 m), although they can be found in much shallower depths. Large congregations of adult blue rockfish are known to gather at midwater depths and engage in feeding frenzies, gorging on crustaceans, jellyfish, algae, and smaller fish.

Cabezons (*Scorpaenichthys marmoratus*), found in tide pools as well as kelp beds in the Pacific Ocean, have poisonous spines on their fins. Adults spawn on rocky outcrops, after which the males guard the eggs until they hatch. Hatchlings drift out to sea on the current but return to tide pools as juveniles for a period of growth. Later the young fish move back into deep water, where they become adults. Crustaceans, mollusks, and small fish make up their diets. The sculpins are relatives of the cabezons and can be found in rocky-bottom areas.

Rocky reefs and kelp beds are also homes to sheepheads, members of family Labridae. Also known as wrasses, fish in this family range from the littoral zone to water that is 180.5 feet (55 m) deep. The California sheephead (*Semicossyphus pulcher*) grows to about three feet (90 cm) at maturity. The most notable features of sheepheads are their steeply sloped foreheads, protruding canine teeth, and powerful jaws. Sheepheads use their strong jaws to crunch into hard-shelled mussels, clams, and even the spiny skins of sea urchins. At night, sheepheads sleep in caves and small crevices in rocks. Some have the ability to secrete a mucous sleeping bag around their bodies that helps prevent predators from detecting them as they rest. The California sheepheads display unusual reproductive strategies. All the fish function as females until they reach about eight years of age. At that time, their ovaries convert into testes and the fish function as males for the remainder of their lives.

Family Clinidae includes the giant kelpfish (*Heterostichus rostratus*), residents of waters from 18 to 70 feet (5.5 to 21.3 m) in depth. Among the kelp, eelgrass, and leafy algae, the slender, blade-shaped bodies of giant kelpfish blend perfectly with their surroundings. These two-feet-long (61-cm) fish can be found from Washington State to Baja California, varying from red to green or brown depending on the color of the local seaweeds. Kelpfish are so well adapted that they can even sway back and forth with the motion of the plants. Giant kelpfish hunt by waiting patiently for unsuspecting small crustaceans, fish, and mollusks to pass near by.

The sea basses, family Serranidie, live in tropical and temperate continental shelf waters. Many are hermaphrodites that start life as females and later change to males. One group of sea bass, the kelp bass (*Paralabrax clathratus*), are generally loners, but when hunting they will congregate to prey on small schools of fish. In a group, kelp bass strategically position themselves to attack the schools from all angles and have been reported to leap high out of the water in pursuit of their prey. Living off the Pacific coast, the adult fish, which grow to 29 inches (72 cm) in length, survive on a diet of smaller fish, squid, and crustaceans. Tiny kelp bass larvae drift along with the plankton, carried by the currents until a blade of kelp strains them from the water. After that, the fish live in close association with the kelp.

Another fish that is commonly found around kelp beds along the California coast is the senorita (*Oxyjulis californica*). A small animal that reaches only about 10 inches (25 cm) in length, senoritas survive by picking external parasites from a variety of surfaces, including the skin of other fish and kelp. When not nibbling tiny invertebrates, they rest with their bodies buried in sand and only their heads protruding.

Conclusion

Over time, different kinds of fish have become highly adapted to life in their particular habitats. Some of the habitats found in the waters over the continental shelves are kelp beds and sea grass meadows, as well as rocky, silty, and sandy substrates. To study the thousands of species found over continental shelves, fish can be divided into groups, depending on their habitats: schooling fish, ground fish, bottom fish, and fish of rocky reefs and kelp beds.

Schooling fish include the little tunny, the Atlantic mackerel, menhaden, bluefish, and barracuda. Schooling is a behavior that increases an individual fish's chance of survival. Some fish school year-round, but others only school during events like spawning or foraging for food. Barracuda and bluefish are both aggressive predators that hunt in schools. Bluefish drive their prey into shallow water, then consume all of them, even regurgitating if necessary to make room for all the food.

Demersal, or groundfish, spend their time within a few feet of the seafloor. Atlantic cod, haddock, pollock, lumpfish, pipefish, and seahorses are just a few of the many species of demersal fish. Lumpfish are unusual in that they have suckers that hold them to rocky substrates, preventing energetic water from washing them away. Seahorses and pipefish lack scales, and their bodies are supported by bony rings. In this family, the father fish play important roles in egg development, caring for and protecting eggs until they are ready to hatch.

Although demersal fish live close to the seafloor, groundfish actually live on it. Groundfish include sole, flounder, turbot, and other flatfish that lie in the sediment with only their eyes exposed. Groundfish are so well camouflaged on the seafloor that they can simply wait for suitable food to swim by, then lunge forward and grab it. Anglerfish are groundfish that possess a special adaptation for catching prey. A lurelike fleshy extension of the dorsal fin dangles in front of this fish's mouth. Any curious fish that swim close enough to check it out will likely become food for the anglerfish. Many species of sharks and rays spend most of their time on the bottom of the continental shelf waters. Sharks, skates, and rays are a group of organisms that lack bony skeletons, like those of most fish. Instead, their skeletal systems are made of cartilage, a soft, flexible material.

Sculpins, rockfish, sheepheads, kelpfish, and sea bass are a few of the fish that live in kelp beds and rocky areas on the continental shelves. In the kelp forest, they can find places to hide from predators, as well as an ample supply of food. As critical links in the kelp and rocky seafloor food webs, these organisms have a tremendous impact on the health of these ecosystems. All are specially adapted for the places where they live. Kelpfish resemble kelp so much that they actually sway to and fro in the water, just like kelp plants. California sheepheads have the amazing ability to change sexes when breeding time arrives, ensuring there will always be enough mates for all females.

6

ℐ Reptiles, Birds, and Mammals
Complex Vertebrates on the Continental Shelf

ertebrates, animals that have backbones, include fish as well *as amphibians, reptiles, birds,* and *mammals.* To many people, the air-breathing marine creatures are some of the sea's best-known inhabitants. All the sea vertebrates are descendents of organisms that lived on land, so they share many of the traits of familiar terrestrial animals, such as respiratory systems that include lungs. Despite their terrestrial ancestors, marine vertebrates are as fit for sea life as any fish.

Reptiles, birds, and mammals generally occupy the highest levels of food chains in marine environments. With their large size and relatively small number of predators, these animals are free to move through their environment in search of prey. In addition, vertebrates are intelligent animals that are equipped with a variety of sensory organs, giving them advantages in their ecosystems that many invertebrates lack.

Marine Reptiles

The kinds of reptiles that can be found living in any part of the continental shelf depends on several factors, including geographical location and climate. The two most common types of sea reptiles found in continental shelf waters are sea turtles and sea snakes. Because they are cold-blooded animals, populations of both reptiles decrease dramatically as one travels from the Tropics toward the poles.

Even though they are large, heavy animals, sea turtles move almost effortlessly through their marine environments. Capable of remaining submerged for as long as three hours, sea turtles are superbly adapted for their marine lifestyles. Five species of sea turtles spend some, or all, of their time in waters of the continental shelves: the Atlantic leatherback (*Dermochelys coriacea*), the Atlantic loggerhead (*Caretta*

caretta), Ridley's sea turtle (*Lepidochelys kempi*), the Atlantic hawksbill (*Eretmochelys imbricata*), and the green sea turtle (*Chelonia mydas*). All five groups of turtles are endangered, and their populations are small.

The green sea turtle can weigh as much as 400 pounds (181 kg). Feeding on turtle grass and manatee grass, green sea turtles spend most of their lives in shallow continental shelf waters. When it is time to breed, they travel more than 1,000 miles (1,609.3 km) to mate and lay their eggs. The largest nesting site in the Western Hemisphere is at Tortuguero, Costa Rica. The Atlantic hawksbill sea turtle is common near coral reefs but swims in other continental shelf waters as well. With an orange, brown, or yellow carapace that measures up to 35.8 inches (91 cm), the hawksbill can weigh 100 to 150 pounds (40 to 60 kg). Named for its hawklike jaw, this turtle uses it narrow mouth to reach into cracks and crevices between rocks and corals to pull out sponges, octopuses, and shrimp. Although endangered in all habitats, some still build nests on beaches of the Caribbean.

The Atlantic leatherback can be found from the Tropics to subarctic zones. Lacking a true bony shell, this species of turtle is protected by a hard, leatherlike carapace that may be black or brown. Leatherbacks have delicate jaws that are designed for eating soft prey like jellyfish. Even on a diet made up of animals that are primarily composed of water, leatherbacks reach impressive weights of 700 to 1,600 pounds (317.5 to 725.8 kg). Often smaller than the leatherback, the Atlantic loggerhead, which has a true shell, weighs up to 1,200 pounds (544.3 kg). Swimming in nearshore waters of the eastern United States, Argentina, the Caribbean, and the Gulf of Mexico, loggerheads, named for their unusually large heads, have shells that are red or brown. Kemp's ridley is a tropical species that is the most endangered of the sea turtles. Also the smallest by sea turtle standards, the Kemp's ridley only reaches weights of 100 pounds (45.36 kg). Ranging in color from gray to olive green, the Kemp's ridley sea turtle visits mangroves, estuaries, and other shallow water habitats to feed. The only major breeding site of this turtle is a narrow stretch of sandy beach at Rancho Nuevo, Mexico.

Marine Reptile Anatomy

Reptiles are not usually associated with marine environments. In fact, of the 6,000 known species of reptiles, only about 1 percent inhabits the sea. Members of this select group include lizards, crocodiles, turtles, and snakes. Each of these organisms shares many of the same anatomical structures that are found in all reptiles: They are cold-blooded, air-breathing, scaled animals that reproduce by internal fertilization. Yet, to live in salt water, this subgroup has evolved some special adaptations not seen in terrestrial reptiles.

In turtles, the shell is the most unique feature. The lightweight, streamline shape of the shell forms a protective enclosure for the vital organs. The ribs and backbone of the turtle are securely attached to the inside of the shell. The upper part of the shell, the carapace, is covered with horny plates that connect to the shell's bottom, the plastron. Extending out from the protective shell are the marine turtle's legs, which have been modified into paddle-like flippers capable of propelling it at speeds of up to 35 miles per hour (56 kph) through the water. These same legs are cumbersome on land, making the animals slow and their movements awkward.

Most air-breathing vertebrates cannot drink salty water because it causes dehydration and kidney damage. Seawater contains sodium chloride and other salts in concentrations three times greater than blood and body fluids. Many marine reptiles drink seawater, so their bodies rely on special salt-secreting glands to handle the excess salt. To reduce the load of salt in body fluids, these glands produce and excrete fluid that is twice as salty as seawater. The glands work very quickly, processing and getting rid of salt about 10 times faster than kidneys. Salt glands are located on the head, often near the eyes.

There are more than 50 species of sea snakes that thrive in marine environments. Sea snakes possess adaptations such as nasal valves and close-fitting scales around the mouth that keep water out during diving. Flattened tails that look like small paddles

Sea snakes, such as the one in the lower color insert on page C-5, favor warm tropical waters, rarely venturing into cool seas. Three of the five families of sea snakes are found in tropical continental shelf waters: Hydrophiidae (true sea snakes), Laticaudidae (sea kraits), and Acrochordidae (file snakes). The Hydrophiidae, the largest group, produce venom that they deliver to prey with front fangs. This group of snakes rarely emerges on land, mating and giving birth to their live young in the water. Members of Hydrophiidae include the olive sea snake and the yellow-bellied sea snake.

easily propel these reptiles through the water. The lungs in sea snakes are elongated, muscular air sacs that are able to store oxygen. In addition, sea snakes can take in oxygen through the skin. Their adaptations to the marine environment enable sea snakes to stay submerged from 30 minutes up to two hours; however, this ability comes at a cost. Because marine snakes routinely swim to the surface to breathe, they use more energy and have higher metabolic rates than land snakes. To balance their high energy consumption, they require more food than their terrestrial counterparts.

Finally, crocodiles usually occupy freshwater, but there are some species that live in brackish water (in between salt water and freshwater) and salt water. These animals have salivary glands that have been modified to excrete salt. Their tails are flattened for side-to-side swimming and their toes possess well-developed webs. Saltwater crocodiles are equipped with valves at the back of the throat that enable them to open their mouths and feed underwater without flooding their lungs.

The olive sea snake (*Aipysurus laevis*) lives in tropical waters, often around coral reefs. Averaging 3.9 feet (1.2 m) in length, adults can reach lengths of six feet (1.8 m). The body of an olive sea snake is round and stout, varying in color from brown to purplish brown, with a creamy white, flattened tail that is trimmed with a brown ridge on the dorsal surface. The tail contains cells that are sensitive to the movement of light, enabling the animal to detect predators that approach when it is feeding. To find food, an olive sea snake moves slowly among seaweeds looking for fish, fish eggs, cuttlefish, and crabs. To kill, it constricts its prey in a tight hold while inject-ing venom with its fangs.

Courtship for olive sea snakes takes place in open water, but mating occurs on the seafloor. Males compete fiercely for the females, who are generally the larger of the sexes. Two to five young are born alive and grow quickly, reaching sexual maturity in five years. The life span of an olive sea snake is about 15 years.

The yellow-bellied sea snake (*Pelamis platurus*) inhabits waters from the Gulf of California to Ecuador. Dark on the dorsal side, the snake has a yellow or cream-colored ventral surface. Lying at the water's surface, a solitary yellow-bellied sea snake may swim slowly, mimicking a single piece of sea-weed, or join other snakes in a floating mass. If an unsuspect-ing fish mistakes either for drifting wood or algae, it quickly becomes a snake's meal. Thousands of yellow-bellied sea snakes can be found lying in calm waters, especially in areas where currents converge.

Seabirds

Making up 3 percent of all bird species, seabirds are highly adapted for their marine lives. Seabirds live on diets of marine organisms and spend most of their time in or over the water. In the waters of the continental shelf, some of the most common families of seabirds include the penguins, auks, shearwaters, petrels, boobies, cormorants, frigatebirds, and jaegers.

Birds in the family Spheniscidae, the penguins, do not fly but use their wings as flippers for swimming. On land they either shuffle in an upright walking position or slide on their bellies. Penguins depend on their keen eyesight to hunt for small animals like krill and other crustaceans in the water.

Penguins are natives of the Southern Hemisphere, living in Antarctica, South America, Africa, Australia, New Zealand, and the Galápagos Islands. A penguin is protected from the cold by a tightly packed layer of feathers and a thick layer of fat as insulation. Most have the familiar white and black col-oration, but there are some species that have yellow or orange markings on them.

The largest species of penguin is the emperor penguin (*Aptenodytes forsteri*), shown in the upper color insert on page C-6. This diving bird can plunge to depths of more than 1,700 feet (518.2 m). Weighing as much as 80 pounds (36.29 kg) and standing four feet (1.2 m) tall, emperor penguins live and breed in the Antarctic. The female lays one egg, which she and the male take turns incubating.

Birds in the family Alcidae, the auks, can use their wings for both flying and swimming. The thick bodies of these Northern Hemisphere residents are either gray or black and white. Most breed in colonies on sea cliffs and rocky slopes, although some species nest in trees. The Atlantic puffin (*Fratercula arctica*), is a medium-sized, heavy bird whose bill changes from a dull, drab winter color to bright multi-colors in the summer. Nesting occurs in Labrador, Newfoundland, the eastern coast of Canada, and northern Europe.

The horned puffin (*Fratercula corniculata*), which is about the size of a pigeon, has a black and white body, a white face, and a small black horn above the eyes. Shown in the lower color insert on page C-6, these birds have orange feet and legs, as well as a large, red-tipped orange bill that make them easy to identify. The horned puffin winters in the ocean off the coast from Alaska to Washington. In the spring, pairs move to shore to breed. When nesting time arrives, the female lays a solitary egg in a hole on the ground or in an opening between large rocks or boulders of cliffs.

A diverse group of birds, family Procellariidae, includes shearwaters, large petrels, and fulmars. Each member of the family has nostrils that are fused into a single tube that runs along the top of its bill. This tube is an adaptation that enables the bird to drink salt water and dispose of the salt. Salt accumulates inside the specialized tube, then the bird sneezes it out. Fulmars are very gull-like in appearance and have heavy bills. The northern fulmar (*Fulmarus glacialis*) is the most common type of tube-nose bird in the northern latitudes, and it breeds in Alaska. All other fulmars build nests in the Southern Hemisphere. The northern fulmar is a gray-necked, yellow-billed bird with dark wings.

Shearwaters are drab-colored birds that have wingspans of about 45 inches (114.3 cm). They live on krill and small fish plucked from the surface of the water. Expert long-distance fliers, shearwaters nest in burrows on offshore islands around the world. The short-tailed shearwater (*Puffinus tenuirostris*) is sooty brown dorsally with a pale ventral surface and a wingspan more than three feet (0.9 m). Breeding occurs on the coasts and islands of southeastern Australia, but birds can be sighted along the Pacific coast of North America.

Named for Saint Peter because of their habit of walking on the water as Saint Peter is said to have done, the petrels are members of the family Hydrobatidae. Found worldwide, they are the smallest representatives of the tube-nose birds. Birds in this family, which includes both migratory and nonmigratory species, are dark brown or black with slender bills and long legs that seem too large proportionally for their bodies. Leach's storm petrel (*Oceanodroma leucorhoa*) has a deeply forked tail and white patch on its rear. With a wingspan of only 19 inches (48.3 cm), this small bird is adept at quick, darting maneuvers and fast changes in direction. Breeding occurs along the coasts and islands of the Pacific, from the Aleutians to Baja California, and in the North Atlantic from Labrador to Maine. The birds spend the winter months in tropical seas.

Diving petrels, members of the family Pelecanoididae, have wingspans about 15 inches (38.1 cm) wide. Dark on the dorsal side and light ventrally, a diving petrel flies close to the water with its wings constantly in motion. When in pursuit of prey, the bird may dive directly into an oncoming wave or straight into the water. The common diving petrel (*Pelecanoides urinatrix*), widespread around the southern oceans, has a brown-back, mottled throat and blue legs.

Members of family Sulidae are referred to as boobies in the Tropics and gannets in northern waters. Like the blue-footed boobies shown in the upper color insert on page C-7, these birds have heavy bodies with short, stout legs, long wedge-shaped tails, and pointed wings. To catch prey, they dive from high above the water and continue to chase it underwater. Air sacks located under their skin cushion the impact of the dive and provide buoyancy.

The masked booby (*Sula dactylatra*) is the largest member of the booby family, slightly less than three feet (0.9 m) in length with a wingspan of around five feet (1.5 m). Coloration is white with brown wings, long, pointed orange bills, and black masks that surround their eyes. The masked booby breeds in the Bahamas and West Indies, making nests in depressions on the ground. Each female deposits one or two eggs, then both parents incubate the eggs with their feet. Even if two eggs are laid, only one chick survives. The second egg may be a backup, in case the first one does not hatch. If both eggs hatch, the older chick forces the younger one from the nest. The parents, realizing they can only care for one chick, move out of the way to allow the older chick to dispose of its sibling.

The cormorants and shags are members of the family Phalacrocoracidae, birds with long necks, hooked bills, elongated bodies and necks, and four webbed toes that point forward. As shown in the lower color insert on page C-6, the coloration of a cormorant is generally dark with a metallic sheen. Cormorants and shags have adjustable, internal air sacs that allow them to modify their buoyancy so they can either swim on the surface or underwater. Their wings are not completely waterproof, so the birds must spend some time on land allowing their feathers to air dry. The pelagic cormorant (*Phalacrocorax pelagicus*), a dark-colored bird, can be seen drying its wings along the Pacific coastline from California to Alaska.

Using aerial assault, birds in the family Fregatidae are pirates that rob other birds of their catches. Commonly known as frigatebirds, these animals are poor swimmers that lack waterproofing on their wings. If they feed from the sea, they swoop down toward the ocean surface and pick up their prey in their long, hooked bills. More often, they steal food from other birds. With wingspans that can be over seven feet (2.1 m) in width, these birds nest in large groups in mangrove trees. The magnificent frigatebird (*Fregata magnificens*) is black, but in breeding season the male develops a bright red throat pouch. The species breeds in mangrove islands off the coast of Florida, and in the tropical Atlantic, eastern Pacific, and Gulf of Mexico.

Closely related to gulls, the family Stercorariidae includes birds that only come ashore to breed. Although generally gull-like in their overall appearance, these birds are more robust and powerful looking than gulls. Members of this family, which includes skuas and jaegers, survive by stealing food from other birds, but they will also raid the nest of other birds, consuming their eggs and young. The great skua (*Stercorarius skua*), a large, dark bird with white blocks on its wings, nests in Iceland and on islands north of Britain. During the winter, it can be found off the North Atlantic coast.

Marine Bird Anatomy

Birds are warm-blooded vertebrates that have feathers to insulate and protect their bodies. In most species of birds, feathers are also important adaptations for flying. As a general rule, birds devote a lot of time and energy to keeping their feathers waterproof in a process called preening. During preening, birds rub their feet, feathers, and beaks with oil produced by the preen gland near their tail.

The strong, lightweight bones of birds are especially adapted for flying. Many of the bones are fused, resulting in the rigid type of skeleton needed for flight. Although birds are not very good at tasting or smelling, their senses of hearing and sight are exceptional. They maintain a constant, relatively high body temperature and a rapid rate of metabolism. To efficiently pump blood around their bodies, they have a four-chambered heart.

Like marine reptiles, marine birds have glands that remove excess salt from their bodies. Although the structure and purpose of the salt gland is the same in all marine birds, its location varies by species. In most marine birds, salt accumulates in a gland near the nostrils and then oozes out of the bird's body through the nasal openings.

The term *seabird* is not scientific but is used to describe a wide range of birds whose lifestyles are associated with the

Marine Mammals

Marine mammals are a diverse group of large, active animals. Worldwide, there are about 4,000 different species of mammals that live in oceans. Some, including harbor seals or bottlenose dolphins, are limited to certain areas such as continental shelves, coral reefs, or estuary systems. Others, like humpback whales and killer whales, travel around the globe.

The marine mammals found in continental shelf waters can be divided into several groups. Otters, members of the weasel family, form a small group of nearshore mammals. Seals, animals with finlike flippers, include sea lions and walruses. The plankton-feeding baleen whales include some of the largest mammals on Earth. Toothed whales, a group that includes dolphins, are carnivores. Dugongs and manatees are the only members of a very small group of animals that are distantly related to elephants.

ocean. Some seabirds never get further out into the ocean than the surf water. Many seabirds are equipped with adaptations of their bills, legs, and feet. Short, tweezerlike bills can probe for animals that are near the surface of the sand or mud, while long, slender bills reach animals that burrow deeply. For wading on wet soil, many seabirds have lobed feet, while those who walk through mud or shallow water have long legs and feet with wide toes.

Other marine birds are proficient swimmers and divers who have special adaptations for spending time in water. These include wide bodies that have good underwater stability, thick layers of body fat for buoyancy, and dense plumage for warmth. In swimmers, the legs are usually located near the posterior end of the body to allow for easy maneuvers, and the feet have webs or lobes between the toes.

All marine birds must come to the shore to breed and lay their eggs. Breeding grounds vary from rocky ledges to sandy beaches. More than 90 percent of marine birds are colonial and require the social stimulation of other birds to complete the breeding process. Incubation of the eggs varies from one species to the next, but as a general rule the length of incubation correlates to the size of the egg: Large eggs take longer to hatch than small ones do.

Marine Mammal Anatomy

Mammals are warm-blooded vertebrates that have hair and breathe air. All females of this group have milk-producing mammary glands with which to feed their young. Mammals also have a diaphragm that pulls air into the lungs and a four-chambered heart for efficient circulation of blood. The teeth of mammals are specialized by size and shape for particular uses.

Marine mammals are subdivided into four categories: cetaceans, animals that spend their entire lives in the ocean; sirenians, herbivorous ocean mammals; pinnipeds, web-footed mammals; and marine otters. Animals in all four categories have the same characteristics as terrestrial mammals, as well as some special adaptations that enable them to survive in their watery environment.

The cetaceans, which include whales, dolphins, and porpoises, have streamlined bodies, horizontal tail flukes, and paddle-like flippers that enable them to move quickly through the water. Layers of blubber (subcutaneous fat) insulate their bodies and act as storage places for large quantities of energy. Their noses (blowholes) are located on the tops of their heads so air can be inhaled as soon as the organism surfaces above the water.

Manatees and dugongs are the only sirenians. These docile, slow-moving herbivores lack a dorsal fin or hind limbs but are equipped with front limbs that move at the elbow, as well as with a flattened tail. Their powerful tails propel them through the water, while the front limbs act as paddles for steering.

The pinnipeds—seals, sea lions, and walruses—are carnivores that have webbed feet. Although very awkward on land, the pinnipeds are agile and aggressive hunters in the water. This group of marine mammals is protected from the cold by hair and blubber. During deep-water dives, their bodies are able to restrict blood flow to vital organs and slow their heart rates to only a few beats a minute, strategies that reduce oxygen consumption. All pinnipeds come onto land or ice at breeding time.

The sea otters spend their entire lives at sea and only come ashore during storms. They are much smaller than the other marine mammals. Even though otters are very agile swimmers and divers, they are clumsy on shore. Their back feet, which are flipperlike and fully webbed, are larger than their front feet. Internally, their bodies are adapted to deal with the salt in seawater with enlarged kidneys that can eliminate the excess salt.

Otters

The family Mustelidae includes the weasel-like sea otter (*Enhydra lutris*). Living off the western coast of North

America, the sea otter rarely gets out of the ocean. Sea otters spend their days floating on their backs as shown in the lower color insert on page C-7, or diving for food in areas where water is shallower than 130 feet (40 m). Choice morsels, like sea urchins and lobster, are brought to the surface and held in the handlike front paws, where they are consumed. Sometimes sea otters use rocks and other simple tools to crush the shells of their prey.

The brown fur of sea otters is extremely thick, the densest of any mammal. The head is short and broad, with a short snout and stiff whiskers. The front paws are small and round, but the back ones large and webbed. Sea otters spend a lot of their time grooming, spreading the oil that waterproofs their bodies through their coat. Males, which are larger than females, can be almost five feet (1.4 m) long and weigh four to five pounds (two to 2.25 kg).

During breeding season, each male mates with several females. To subdue a chosen mate, the male grabs a female by the nose with his sharp teeth, often leaving it bloody. The noses of most of the older females bear multiple scars, attesting to years as breeding adults. Pups stay close to their mothers, often riding on their stomachs or backs, and may nurse for a period of six months to a year.

Pinnipeds

Members of the families Otariidae (eared seals) and Phocidae (true seals) are collectively known as the pinnipeds, or fin-footed animals. All pinnipeds have similar physical adaptations that give them grace and speed in the water, but make them slow and clumsy on land. To streamline and reduce their drag in water, the bodies of pinnipeds either lack ears or have ears of reduced size and have genitals and teats inside the body. Their limbs are flattened for swimming purposes. Many species of pinnipeds are able to live in extremely cold environments because their bodies are covered with a thick layer of blubber located beneath the skin.

Members of Phocidae, the true seals, lack external ears, but have a very good sense of hearing. Phocidae cannot fold their hind limbs forward, so when they move across the land, they must hop on their bellies while supporting themselves with their front limbs. For this reason they are sometimes nicknamed the "crawling seals." In continental shelf waters, this group includes the bearded seal, largha seal, ringed seal, ribbon seal, gray seal, Weddell seal, crab eater seal, and harp seal.

Those in family Otariidae are known as the eared seals, a group that includes sea lions and fur seals. Otariidae have small external ears and hind limbs that can be folded forward to allow mobility on land. When out of water, the front flippers support the body, which can be walked forward on the hind limbs. This group includes the Antarctic and subantarctic fur seals, Guadalupe fur seal, South American fur seal, Galápagos fur seal, California sea lion, and northern sea lion.

The California sea lion (*Zalophus californianus*) is familiar to many people as the species most often trained in zoos and circuses. An active, vocal animal, the California sea lion is very social, and thousands go ashore, a behavior known as "hauling out," to play, vocalize or just rest. Males, who are robust with large chests, necks, and shoulders, reach lengths of 7.8 feet (2.4 m) and weigh 860 pounds (110 kg), but females are less than half their size. The hair on males is usually black, with tan areas on the face, while females and juveniles are gray to silver.

The gray seal (*Halichoerus grypus*) is also a gregarious animal, congregating on beaches and floes of pack ice. Most gray seals are found in the North Atlantic Ocean along the northeast coast of North America, and near Iceland, Norway, and the British Isles. Males, who have brown spotted coats, can reach a length of 8.5 feet (2.6 m) and a weight of 770 pounds (350 kg). Females generally have tan spotted coats and grow to about one-third the size of males.

The Hawaiian monk seals (*Monachus schauinslandi*), residents of the Hawaiian Islands, are solitary animals. When hauled out on the beach, monk seals space themselves widely to avoid conflicts. Males can weigh 35 to 40 pounds (16 to 18 kg) and grow to 6.9 feet (2.1 m) in length. Generally, a Hawaiian monk seal, like the one in the upper color insert on page C-8, has tan to gray fur, a slender body, short flippers, and a small head. Unlike most other species of pinnipeds, the males are slightly smaller than females.

Whales

Whales, or cetaceans, include more than 80 different species of animals. Cetaceans are long, streamlined mammals that move through the water under the power of strong flippers. Well adapted for life in the sea, their external ears, mammary glands, and genitals are located within the body so they will not create drag as the animals swim. Some cetaceans are solitary, but others are highly social, living in groups called pods. Several of the cetaceans migrate, and their paths and periods of migration vary by species. Generally, these organisms are divided into two groups based on their feeding adaptations: toothed whales and baleen whales.

Suborder Odontoceti, the toothed whales, includes sperm whales, beaked dolphins, beluga whales, and porpoises. Toothed whales are carnivores that feed on a variety of fish, invertebrates, and mammals, depending on the species. Baleen whales, a group that strains tiny zooplankton from the water, is made up of four families, which are collectively known as the mysticetes.

Beluga whales and narwhals are close relatives that spend some of their lives in continental shelf waters but also dive in deep ocean regions. Belugas (*Delphinapterus leucas*), also known as "sea canaries" because of their frequent vocalizations, are abundant in the Arctic and subarctic regions. Measuring up to 16 feet (4.9 m) and weighing as much as 3,500 pounds (1,600 kg), the rounded, white bodies of beluga whales are impressive sights. A hump or bulge on a beluga's head is called a melon, an oil-filled structure that scientists believe is used to focus or enhance sound waves. The whales can change the shape of the melon by moving the air in it to different cavities. In the summers, belugas tend to move close to shore and even into estuaries, traveling back offshore in the winter. These social animals live in pods and enjoy communicating.

The family Delphinidae, the ocean dolphins, is a large one, but all its members have some common characteristics. Colored in bold black and white patterns, the ocean dolphins have dorsal fins and notched flukes, or tails, as shown in the lower color insert on page C-8. Some of the animals included in this group are the bottlenose dolphin, striped dolphin, spinner dolphin, Atlantic spotted dolphin, killer whale, and pilot whale.

Bottlenose dolphins (*Tursiops truncates*) live in temperate and tropical waters worldwide. Smaller than most other whales, male bottlenose dolphins grow to 12 feet (3.7 m) long and weigh up to 1,100 pounds (500 kg). Their color is gray, with dark tones on the dorsal side and light ones on the ventral surface. Very social animals, bottlenose dolphins form pods that are made up of related animals.

Spinner dolphins (*Stennella longirostris*), named for their ability to spin during acrobatic jumps from the water, are slender, with long thin beaks, sloping foreheads, and a stripe that runs from the eyes to the flippers. An adult measures about seven feet (2.1 m) long, and weighs between 100 and 165 pounds (45 and 75 kg). The pods of spinner dolphins are loose associations of a few key members as well as individuals who join the group temporarily. It is not unusual for a pod to spend time with other sea animals, like pilot whales, spotted dolphins, or tuna. Spinner dolphins may use their pectoral fins to reach out and stroke one another, acts that strengthen the social bonds between them. Described as a pan tropical species, spinner dolphins are found between the Tropics of Cancer and Capricorn.

Body Temperature

Animals that are described as warm blooded, or endothermic, maintain a constant internal temperature, even when exposed to extreme temperatures in their environment. In mammals, this internal temperature is about 97°F (36°C), while in birds, it is warmer, around 108°F (42°C).

Warm-blooded animals have developed several physiological and behavioral modifications that help regulate body temperature. Since their bodies generate heat by converting food into energy, they must take in enough food to fuel a constant body temperature. Once heat is produced, endotherms conserve it with insulating adaptations such as hair, feathers, or layers of fat. In extreme cold, they also shiver, a mechanism that generates additional heat.

Heart rate and rate of respiration in warm-blooded animals does not depend on the temperature of the surroundings. For this reason, they can be as active on a

The largest member of the Delphinidae family is the killer whale (*Orcinus orca*). Males can grow to lengths of 30 feet (9.1 m) and weigh 12,000 pounds (5,600 kg). The dorsal fins of killer whales are tall and erect, averaging three to six feet (one to 1.8 m) in height. Their colors are bold patterns of black and white, often with the shapes of white saddles on their backs. Unlike most other species of toothed whales, killer whales can tolerate waters of almost any depth and temperature. Some of their favorite prey includes baleen whales, penguins, and seals. These social animals form long-lasting pods that are organized around female leaders. A cosmopolitan marine mammal, the killer whale can be found in oceans around the world, usually going where the prey is most abundant.

Another large member of this group is the long-finned pilot whale (*Globicephala melas*), a 21-foot-long (6.4 m) animal that can weigh 5,000 pounds (2,300 kg). Found on both sides of the North Atlantic Ocean, this whale is primarily black with small amounts of white on its dorsal and ventral sides. Pilot whales have melons on their heads, and dorsal fins that are shaped like the letter *C*. At times, they can be spotted playing in surface waters, or diving for food such as squid and mackerel. A southern subspecies lives in the Antarctic waters, while a northern subspecies travels in an area bordered by eastern Canada and northwestern Europe.

cold winter night as they are during a summer day. This is a real advantage that enables warm-blooded animals to actively look for food year round.

The internal temperature of cold-blooded, or ectothermic, animals is the same as the temperature of their surroundings. In other words, when it is hot outside, they are hot, and when it is cold outside, they are cold. In very hot environments the blood temperature of some cold-blooded animals can rise far above the blood temperature of warm-blooded organisms. Furthermore, their respiration rate is dependent on the temperature of their surroundings. To warm up and speed their metabolism, cold-blooded animals often bask in the sun. Therefore, cold-blooded animals such as fish, amphibians, and reptiles, tend to be much more active in warm environments than in cold conditions.

Although they resemble one another, dolphins and porpoises are not the same animals. True porpoises belong to the family Phocoenidae. Porpoises lack beaks and are the smaller of the two animals. Some members of this family include finless porpoise (*Neophocaena phocaenoides*), harbor porpoise (*Phocoena phocoena*), Burmeister's porpoise (*Phocoena spinipinnis*), and Dall's porpoise (*Phocoenoides dalli*).

The harbor porpoise is a five-foot-long (1.5 m) gray animal that weighs as much as 134 pounds (61 kg). The dorsal fins of harbor porpoises are often spotted with rows of tubercles, knobs that have sensory functions. Each tubercle contains a hairlike structure, a vibrissa, that helps detect vibrations in the water. Not very social, these mammals usually spend their time alone or in very small groups. Harbor porpoises can be found in several different parts of the ocean, including the shelf waters, harbors, and bays along both coasts of the United States, and the eastern and northern coasts of Europe.

Baleen whales feed by engulfing water and straining it through food-catching sieves called baleen plates, shown in Figure 6.1. Made of a flexible tissue that is similar to fingernail, baleen plates grow from bases in the roof of a whale's mouth. Baleen whales feed on zooplankton and small schooling fish by engulfing large volumes of water and expelling it through the baleen, trapping organisms inside. Some species take in sea water in large gulps, while others swim with their mouths open. Most baleen whales can open their mouths incredibly wide because their throats contain long, accordion-like, expandable pleats. Baleen whales in continental shelf waters include humpback whales, pygmy whales, right whales, blue whales, and minke whales.

The humpback whale (*Megaptera novaeangliae*) is 40 to 50 feet (12.9 to 15.2 meters) long and weighs up to 55 tons (50,000 kg). A typical humpback is black on the dorsal side, with a white ventral surface, extremely long flippers, and torpedo-shaped body. The head and mouth are both large, the whale's eyes are set above the ends of the mouth, and the small ear slits are located behind and below the eyes. Tubercles are located near the blowhole on the top of its head as well as on the upper and lower jaws. Like many species of whales, male humpbacks

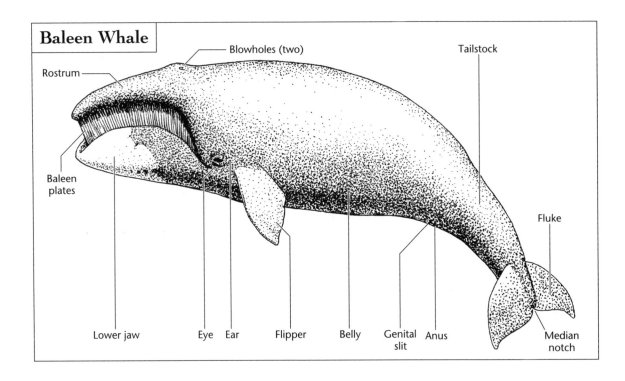

Baleen Whale

Rostrum

Blowholes (two)

Tailstock

Baleen plates

Fluke

Lower jaw   Eye   Ear   Flipper   Belly   Genital   Anus   Median
                                                  slit   notch

sing long, complex songs that can last for hours. The exact function of their songs is not known, but they are believed to be associated with mating. Some songs seem to attract females while others warn off other males. Humpbacks are found in oceans all over the world. Migratory animals, they feed during the summer in mid- to high-latitudes and calve during the winter months near the Tropics.

The minke whale (*Balaenoptera acutorostrata*) is the second smallest of the baleen whales, measuring about 32.8 feet (10 m) in length. The minke's head is triangular and pointed with a very narrow and pointed snout. The dorsal fin is tall and sickle-shaped, and the body is black, gray, or brown on the dorsal surface and light colored on the ventral side.

Minke whales are most often solitary animals, although they occasionally form small groups. When food is plentiful, congregations of several hundred whales may form in the feeding grounds. To communicate with each other, minke whales use low-frequency sounds that can travel

Fig. 6.1   Baleen whales have two blowholes and large mouths filled with baleen plates.

long distances under water. Sometimes, they chase schools of small fish like sardines and herring, swimming beneath and scooping them up in their open mouths. Like humpback whales, the throats of minkes are pleated and expandable. Minkes range worldwide, usually spending the colder months of each year in tropical climes and the warmer months in northern latitudes.

Sirenians

Sirenians are a small group of marine mammals that includes manatees and dugongs, shown in Figure 6.2. Large front flippers guide their stout bodies slowly through the water. These slow-moving herbivores graze on sea grass, pulling it up with their thick upper lips. To keep out water, their nostrils close during feeding.

The West Indian manatee (*Trichechus manatus*) lives in continental shelf waters along eastern North and South America. This gray animal has tough, thickened skin with interspersed hairs. Females are larger than males, growing to 13.5 feet (4.1 m) and weighing 3,000 pounds (1,400 kg). Manatees are not very social, and the closest relationships form between mother and calf. Females produce one or two calves after 12 months of gestation, and nurse them for 18 months. Manatees can live 60 to 70 years.

Shy and retiring, dugongs spend their days feeding in shallow waters of reefs and coastlines of the Western Pacific and Indian Oceans. These relatives of manatees can reach 11 feet (3.4 m) in length and weigh up to 2,200 pounds (1,000 kg). Dugongs have a thick layer of blubber under their skin, a feature that gives them a round-shouldered look. Their tails are triangular and their snouts are broad and trunklike.

Dugongs graze on sea grass blades and dig up their roots, behavior that has earned them the nickname of "sea pigs." Females give birth to one calf every three or four years after a gestation period of 13 months. A calf nurses for two years, always remaining close enough to its mother to touch her. In her lifetime, which averages about 55 years, a female produces only five or six offspring.

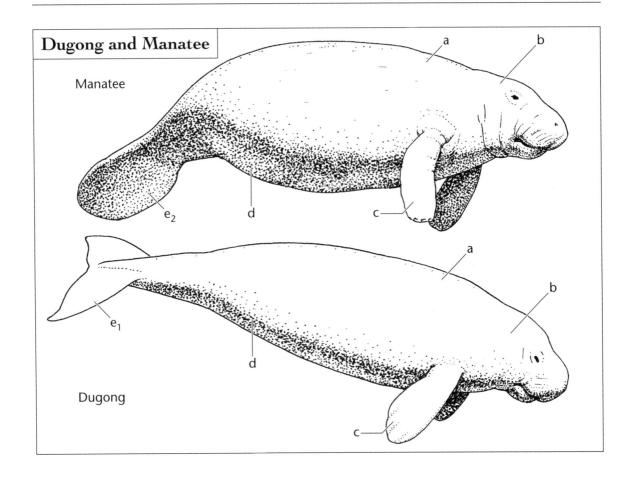

Dugong and Manatee

Manatee

Dugong

Dugongs are so shy that not much is known about their social interactions. Attempts to observe dugongs disturbs their natural behavior and kindles their curiosity in the observers. They are usually spotted singly or in small groups of six to eight animals. Within a group there seems to be no leader or organized social structure.

Conclusion

Reptiles, birds, and mammals are three groups of vertebrates found in continental shelf waters. All are descended from terrestrial ancestors, but have developed elaborate modifications that enable them to succeed in the sea. These vertebrates have

Fig. 6.2   Dugongs and manatees are highly adapted to aquatic life. The body hair (a) is sparse, there are no external earflaps (b), and the forelimbs are modified as strong paddles (c). On the posterior end, there are no hind limbs (d), and the tail is flattened, like the fluke of a whale in dugongs (e_1) or the paddle of a beaver in manatees (e_2).

retained lungs, so those who swim must surface often to breath.

Sea turtles and sea snakes are marine reptiles that move through the water with ease, but are clumsy on land. Most common in warm climates, sea turtles swim close to shore or out to deep water as their breeding cycles and feeding needs dictate. Only female sea turtles ever leave the water, and they do so to lay their eggs. Sea snakes are limited to tropical zones, where they feed on small fish. Most are slow swimmers, so they must lie in wait for their prey. Once they capture prey, sea snakes inject it with venom, then swallow the animal whole.

Seabirds vary tremendously in their adaptations and lifestyles. All depend on the sea for their food but return to land to lay and incubate eggs. Some, like penguins, no longer fly because their wings are extremely modified for swimming. Shearwaters and fulmars fly over the water and pick up prey that are swimming near the surface, while diving petrels, boobies, and gannets plunge into the sea after their prey. Frigatebirds, jaegers, and skuas steal food from other birds and rob their nests.

Marine mammals living in shelf waters include otters, seals, sea lions, whales, porpoises, and dolphins. All are equipped with streamlined bodies that move easily through the water and layers of fat or dense hair to keep them warm. Many, like marine otters, killer whales, and porpoises, are carnivores at the top of their food chains, but others, including manatees and dugongs, are slow-moving and gentle herbivores.

7

Safeguarding the Continental Shelf

Anyone who has waded knee-deep into the ocean has stood in the waters of the continental shelf. Beginning just below the intertidal zone, the continental shelf extends from the coast to the edge of the continental slope, a point where the seafloor drops away steeply. Shelf waters include all of those nearshore regions that border the edges of the landmasses. From the perspective of a wader, the area may look infinite, extending to the horizon. However, the continental shelf makes up only a small part of the ocean, about 8 percent, or an area equal to the size of Asia.

Despite its relatively small size, the continental shelf is a highly productive zone that supports more life than the rest of the open ocean. The key to such productivity is the high levels of nutrients that constantly wash in from land. Nutrients provide food for phytoplankton, macroalgae, sea grasses, and kelp. These producers form the base of a food web that includes organisms ranging in size from microscopic zooplankton to humpback whales.

Most species of fish spend at least some portion of their lives in shelf waters because of the abundance of food there. Because so many fish live near the shore, shelf waters have always served as the rich fishing sites for humans. Today, as much as 90 percent of the harvest of fish and shellfish still comes from these regions.

Humans have also depended on the nearshore seas conduits for trade and travel. Shipping lanes move barges and freighters up and down the coasts of all continents. International trade requires that continental shelf water accommodate ships from overseas, and the activities of military organizations involve ships, submarines, and oceanic research.

The intrinsic values of continental shelf waters far exceed their usefulness to people. As the parts of the sea that receive nutrients from land, nearshore waters are the places where freshwater and sediment are integrated into the marine environment. Currents, tides, and waves quickly incorporate incoming waters and disperse their loads of soil, nutrients, and organic material.

Some of the nutrients entering the relatively shallow areas are quickly consumed by the lush populations of nearshore heterotrophs and decomposers. This link in the food chain frees the nutrients, making them available to small animals and plants. The types of plants found on the shelves include thick meadows of sea grasses, canopied forests of kelp, and dense stands of macroalgae. These plants provide ideal habitats for a variety of marine animals including fish, shellfish, turtles, sea birds, and mammals, serving as places to hide, spawn, and feed in relative safety.

A Vulnerable Resource

The continental shelves and their waters have been seriously impacted by the activities of humans. The primary culprit is the rapid growth of human populations along the edges of continents. In the 30-year period from 1970 to 2000, the most recent time for which data is available, the population of the northeast coast of the United States increased 50 percent. With such staggering growth has come an equally staggering set of problems.

Pollution along the coasts affects the quality of the neighboring marine environments, changing their structure and chemistry. Fertilizers, pesticides, and sediments that reach shallow continental shelf waters have far-reaching consequences. Animals that consume pesticides suffer from reduced productivity. Algae nourished by fertilizers create unnaturally thick masses of green cells that serve as food for oxygen-depleting populations of bacteria. Silt clouds the water, covers filter-feeding animals, and coats the surfaces of grass and algae. In addition, coastal construction projects such as the development of marinas, jetties, and sea walls alter nearshore environments and reduce the wealth of marine life there.

Each life form in the continental shelf waters is a vital important link in the food chain, and the loss of even one harms the entire ecosystem. Consequently, it is in the best interest of humans to protect each species. In the past, when the public perceived the nearshore seas to be bottomless treasure pits hunters reduced the populations of whales to dangerously low numbers. Heavy fishing damaged the once plentiful populations of fish and destructive fishing techniques destroyed many continental shelf habitats.

Solutions and Answers

The good news is that scientists and laymen alike are learning more about the delicate ecosystems of the continental shelves. Most of this knowledge comes from marine research, which has been boosted by the technological advances of the last 20 years. Through the work of scientists operating equipment like undersea cameras and deep-water submersibles, the public is getting a picture of the nearshore sea as a vulnerable natural resource that needs protection. By finding out more about the ways marine systems operate, scientists can determine where and when human activities are causing problems. This kind of information makes it possible to minimize the kinds of activities that have negative impacts on the marine environment.

Since every landmass is bordered by a continental shelf, international cooperation is essential if a long-term solution is to be found. Proposals to limit fishing and eliminate fishing techniques that damage bottom habitats are currently under consideration on a global scale. In addition, marine sanctuaries, protected places in nearshore waters, are being established around the world.

One of the first types of continental shelf environments to garner international protection was the coral reef. Loss of coral reef organisms has clearly been linked to overfishing and pollution, prompting many countries to protect their reefs as national treasures. In recent years, sea grass beds and kelp forests have also been recognized as habitats that need to be protected. These strides suggest a change of attitude and a trend to safeguard shelf waters with the same kind of consideration that has been given fragile terrestrial environments.

The key to success seems to be finding a balance between behavior that wisely uses the resources of shallow, nearshore oceans and activities that damage them. Each of the developed nations bordering these submerged lands is engaged in writing policies to govern the use of continental shelf waters, and overseers such as the United Nations are encouraging and coordinating the international efforts. The key to success in this quest may lie in education. Only when all those involved understand the value of conserving and protecting these environments will the future of the nearshore seas, and their inhabitants, be secure.

Glossary

A

algal bloom The rapid growth of cyanobacteria or algae populations that results in large mats of organisms floating in the water.

amphibian A cold-blooded, soft-skinned vertebrate whose eggs hatch into larvae that metamorphose into adults.

animal An organism capable of voluntary movement that consumes food rather than manufacturing it from carbon compounds.

anterior The region of the body that is related to the front or head end of an organism.

appendage A structure that grows from the body of an organism, such as a leg or antenna.

arthropod An invertebrate animal that has a segmented body, joined appendages, and chitinous exoskeleton.

asexual reproduction A type of reproduction that employs means other than the union of an egg and sperm. Budding and binary fission are forms of asexual reproduction.

autotroph An organism that can capture energy to manufacture its own food from raw materials.

B

binary fission A type of cell division in monerans in which the parent cell separates into two identical daughter cells.

biodiversity The number and variety of life-forms that exist in a given area.

bird A warm-blooded vertebrate that is covered with feathers and reproduces by laying eggs.

bladder In macroalgae, an inflatable structure that holds gases and helps keep blades of the plant afloat.

blade The part of a nonvascular plant that is flattened and leaflike.

brood A type of behavior that enables a parent to protect eggs or offspring as they develop.

budding A type of asexual reproduction in which an offspring grows as a protrusion from the parent.

buoyancy The upward force exerted by a fluid on matter that causes the matter to tend to float.

C

carnivore   An animal that feeds on the flesh of other animals.

chanocyte   A flagellated cell found in the gastrovascular cavity of a sponge that moves water through the pores, into the gastrovascular cavity, and out the osculum (an exit for outflow).

chitin   A tough, flexible material that forms the exoskeletons of arthropods and cell walls of fungi.

chlorophyll   A green pigment, found in all photosynthetic organisms, that is able to capture the Sun's energy.

cilia   A microscopic, hairlike cellular extension that can move rhythmically and may function in locomotion or in sweeping food particles toward an animal's mouth or oral opening.

cnidarian   An invertebrate animal that is radially symmetrical and has a saclike internal body cavity and stinging cells.

cnidocyte   A nematocyst-containing cell found in the tentacles of cnidarians that is used to immobilize prey or defend against predators.

countershading   One type of protective, two-tone coloration in animals in which surfaces that are exposed to light are dark colored and those that are shaded are light colored.

cyanobacteria   A moneran that contains chlorophyll as well as other accessory pigments and can carry out photosynthesis.

D

detritivore   An organism that feeds on dead and decaying matter.

detritus   Decaying organic matter that serves as a source of energy for detritivores.

DNA   Deoxyribonucleic acid, a molecule located in the nucleus of a cell that carries the genetic information that is responsible for running that cell.

dorsal   Situated on the back or upper side of an organism.

E

ecosystem   A group of organisms and the environment in which they live.

endoskeleton   An internal skeleton or support system such as the type found in vertebrates.

energy   The ability to do work.

epidermis   The outer, protective layer of cells on an organism, such as the skin.

exoskeleton   In crustaceans, a hard but flexible outer covering that supports and protects the body.

F

fish A cold-blooded, aquatic vertebrate that has fins, gills, and scales and reproduces by laying eggs that are externally fertilized.

flagellum A long, whiplike cellular extension that is used for locomotion or to create currents of water within the body of an organism.

food chain The path that nutrients and energy follow as they are transferred through an ecosystem.

food web Several interrelated food chains in an ecosystem.

fungus An immobile heterotrophic organism that consumes its food by first secreting digesting enzymes on it, then absorbing the digested food molecules through the cell walls of threadlike hyphae.

G

gastrodermis The layer of cells that lines the digestive cavity of a sponge or cnidarian, and the site at which nutrient molecules are absorbed.

gastropod A class of arthropods that has either one shell or no shells, a distinct head equipped with sensory organs, and a muscular foot.

gill A structure containing thin, highly folded tissues that are rich in blood vessels and serve as the sites where gases are exchanged in aquatic organisms.

glucose A simple sugar that serves as the primary fuel in the cells of most organisms. Glucose is the product of photosynthesis.

H

herbivore An animal that feeds on plants.

hermaphrodite An animal in which both male and female sexual organs are present.

heterotroph An organism that cannot make its own food and must consume plant or animal matter to meet its body's energy needs.

holdfast The rootlike portion of a macroalga that holds the plant to the substrate.

hydrogen bond A weak bond between the positive end of one polar molecule and the negative end of another.

hyphae Filamentous strands that make up the bodies of fungi and form the threadlike extensions that produce digestive enzymes and absorb dissolved organic matter.

I

invertebrate An animal that lacks a backbone, such as a sponge, cnidarian, worm, mollusk, or arthropod.

L

lateral   The region of the body that is along the side of an organism.

lateral line   A line along the side of a fish that connects to pressure-sensitive nerves that enable the fish to detect vibrations in the water.

larva   The newly hatched offspring of an animal that is structurally different from the adult form.

light   A form of electromagnetic radiation that includes infrared, visible, ultraviolet, and X-ray that travels in waves at the speed of 186,281 miles (300,000 km) per second.

M

mammal   A warm-blooded vertebrate that produces living young that are fed with milk from the mother's mammary glands.

mantle   A thin tissue that lies over the organs of a gastropod and secretes the shell.

mesoglea   A jellylike layer that separates the two cell layers in the bodies of sponges and cnidarians.

milt   A fluid produced by male fish that contains sperm and is deposited over eggs laid by the female.

mixotroph   An organism that can use the Sun's energy to make its own food or can consume food.

molt   Periodic shedding of an outer layer of shell, feathers, or hair that allows new growth to occur.

moneran   A simple, one-celled organism that neither contains a nucleus nor membrane-bound cell structures.

motile   Capable of moving from place to place.

N

nematocyst   In cnidarians, a stinging organelle that contains a long filament attached to a barbed tip that can be used in defense or to capture prey.

O

omnivore   An animal that eats both plants and animals.

operculum   In fish, the external covering that protects the gills. In invertebrates, a flap of tissue that can be used to close the opening in a shell, keeping the animal moist and protecting it from predators.

oviparous   An animal that produces eggs that develop and hatch outside the mother's body.

ovoviviparous An animal that produces eggs that develop and hatch within the mother's body, then are extruded.

P

pectoral An anatomical feature, such as a fin, that is located on the chest.

pelvic An anatomical feature, such as a fin, that is located near the pelvis.

photosynthesis The process in which green plants use the energy of sunlight to make nutrients.

plant A nonmotile, multicellular organism that contains chlorophyll and is capable of making its own food.

polar molecule A molecule that has a negatively charged end and a positively charged end.

polychaete A member of a group of worms that has a segmented body and paired appendages.

posterior The region near the tail or hind end of an organism.

productivity The rate at which energy is used to convert carbon dioxide and other raw materials into glucose.

protist A one-celled organism that contains a nucleus and membrane-bound cell structures such as ribosomes for converting food to energy and Golgi apparati for packaging cell products.

R

radula A long muscle used for feeding that is covered with toothlike projections, found in most types of gastropods.

reptile A cold-blooded, egg-laying terrestrial vertebrate whose body is covered with scales.

S

salinity The amount of dissolved minerals in ocean water.

school A group of aquatic animals swimming together for protection or to locate food.

sessile Permanently attached to a substrate and therefore immobile.

setae Hairlike bristles that are located on the segments of polychaete worms.

sexual reproduction A type of reproduction in which egg and sperm combine to produce a zygote.

spawn The act of producing gametes, or offspring, in large numbers, often in bodies of water.

spicule   In sponges, a needle-like, calcified structure located in the body wall that provides support and protection.

spiracle   An opening for breathing, such as the blowhole in a whale or the opening on the head of a shark or ray.

stipe   A stemlike structure in a nonvascular plant.

surface tension   A measure of how easy or difficult it is for molecules of a liquid to stick together due to the attractive forces between them.

swim bladder   A gas-filled organ that helps a fish control its position in the water.

symbiosis   A long-term association between two different kinds of organisms that usually benefits both in some way.

T

territorial behavior   The defense of a certain area or territory by an animal for the purpose of protecting food, a mate, or offspring.

thallus   The body of a macroalgae, made up of the blade, stipe, and holdfast.

V

ventral   Situated on the stomach or lower side of an organism.

vertebrate   A member of a group of animals with backbones, including fish, amphibian, reptiles, birds, and mammals.

viviparous   An animal that gives birth to living offspring.

Z

zooxanthella   A one-celled organism that lives in the tissues of invertebrates such as coral, sponge, or anemone where it carries out photosynthesis.

Further Reading and Web Sites

Books

Banister, Keith, and Andrew Campbell. *The Encyclopedia of Aquatic Life*. New York: Facts On File, 1985. Well written and beautifully illustrated book on all aspects of the ocean and the organisms in it.

Coulombe, Deborah A. *The Seaside Naturalist*. New York: Fireside, 1990. A delightful book for young students who are beginning their study of ocean life.

Davis, Richard A. *Oceanography: An Introduction to the Marine Environment*. Dubuque, Iowa: Wm. C. Brown Publishers, 1991. A text that helps students become familiar with and appreciate the world's oceans.

Dean, Cornelia. *Against the Tide*. New York: Columbia University Press, 1999. An analysis of the impact of humans and nature on the ever-changing beaches.

Ellis, Richard. *Encyclopedia of the Sea*. New York: Alfred A. Knopf, 2000. A factual, yet entertaining, compendium of sea life and lore.

Garrison, Tom. *Oceanography*. New York: Wadsworth Publishing, 1996. An interdisciplinary examination of the ocean for beginning marine science students.

Karleskint, George, Jr. *Introduction to Marine Biology*. Belmont, Calif.: Brooks/Cole-Thompson Learning, 1998. An enjoyable text on marine organisms and their relationships with one another and with their physical environments.

McCutcheon, Scott, and Bobbi McCutcheon. *The Facts On File Marine Science Handbook*. New York: Facts On File, 2003. An excellent resource that includes information on marine physical factors and living things as well as the people who have been important in ocean studies.

Nowak, Ronald M., et al. *Walker's Marine Mammals of the World*. Baltimore, Md.: Johns Hopkins University Press, 2003. An overview on the anatomy, taxonomy, and natural history of the marine mammals.

Pinet, Paul R. *Invitation to Oceanography*. Sudbury, Mass.: Jones and Bartlett Publishers, 2000. Includes explanations of the causes and effects of tides and currents, as well as the origins of ocean habitats.

Prager, Ellen J. *The Sea*. New York: McGraw-Hill, 2000. An evolutionary view of life in the Earth's oceans.

Reeves, Randall R., et al. *Guide to Marine Mammals of the World*. New York: Alfred A. Knopf, 2002. An encyclopedic work on sea mammals accompanied with gorgeous color plates.

Rice, Tony. *Deep Oceans*. Washington, D.C.: Smithsonian Museum Press, 2000. A visually stunning look at life in the deep ocean.

Sverdrup, Keith A., Alyn C. Duxbury, and Alison B. Duxbury. *An Introduction to the World's Oceans*. New York: McGraw Hill, 2003. A comprehensive text on all aspects of the physical ocean, including the seafloor and the ocean's physical properties.

Thomas, David. *Seaweeds*. Washington, D.C.: Smithsonian Museum Press, 2002. Illustrates and describes seaweeds from microscopic forms to giant kelps, explaining how they live, what they look like, and why humans value them.

Thorne-Miller, Boyce, and John G. Catena. *The Living Ocean*. Washington, D.C.: Friends of the Earth, 1991. A study of the loss of diversity in ocean habitats.

Waller, Geoffrey. *SeaLife: A Complete Guide to the Marine Environment*. Washington, D.C.: Smithsonian Institution Press, 1996. A text that describes the astonishing diversity of organisms in the sea.

Web Sites

Bird, Jonathon. *Adaptations for Survival in the Sea*, Oceanic Research Group, 1996. Available online. URL: http://www.oceanicresearch.org/adapspt.html. Accessed March 19, 2004. A summary and review of the educational film of the same name, which describes and illustrates some of the adaptations that animals have for life in salt water.

Buchheim, Jason. "A Quick Course in Ichthyology." Odyssey Expeditions. Available online. URL: http://www.marinebiology.org/fish.htm. Accessed January 4, 2004. A detailed explanation of fish physiology.

"Conservation: Why Care About Reefs?" REN Reef Education Network, Environment Australia. Available online. URL: http://www.reef.edu.au/asp_pages/search.asp. Accessed November 18, 2004. A superb Web site dedicated to the organisms living in and the health of the coral reefs.

Duffy, J. Emmett. "Underwater urbanites: Sponge-dwelling napping shrimps are the only known marine animals to live in colonies that resemble the societies of bees and wasps." *Natural History*. December 2003. Available online. URL: http://www.findarticles.com/cf_dls/m1134/10_111736243/print.jhtml. Accessed January 2, 2004. A readable and fascinating explanation of eusocial behavior in shrimp and other animals.

"Fungus Farming in a Snail." *Proceedings of the National Academy of Science,* 100, no. 26 (December 4, 2003). Available online. URL: http://www.pnas.org/cgi/content/abstract/100/26/15643. A well-written, in-depth analysis of the ways that snails encourage the growth of fungi for their own food.

Gulf of Maine Research Institute Web site. Available online. URL: http://www.gma.org/about_GMA/default.asp. Accessed January 2, 2004. A comprehensive and up-to-date research site on all forms of marine life.

"Habitat Guides: Beaches and Shorelines." eNature. Available online. URL: http://www.enature.com/habitats/show_sublifezone.asp?sublifezoneID=60# Anchor-habitat-49575. Accessed November 21, 2003. A Web site with young people in mind that provides comprehensive information on habitats, organisms, and physical ocean factors.

Huber, Brian T. "Climate Change Records from the Oceans: Fossil Foraminifera." Smithsonian National Museum of Natural History. June 1993. Available online. URL: http://www.nmnh.si.edu/paleo/marine/foraminifera.htm. Accessed December 30, 2003. A concise look at the natural history of foraminifera.

"Index of Factsheets." Defenders of Wildlife. Available online. URL: http://www.kidsplanet.org/factsheets. Accessed November 18, 2004. Various species of marine animals are described on this excellent Web site suitable for both children and young adults.

King County's Marine Waters Web site. Available online. URL: http://splash.metrokc.gov/wlr/waterres/marine/index.htm. Accessed December 2, 2003. A terrific Web site on all aspects of the ocean, emphasizing the organisms that live there.

Mapes, Jennifer. "U.N. Scientists Warn of Catastrophic Climate Changes." National Geographic News. February 6, 2001. Available online. URL: http://news.nationalgeographic.com/news/2001/02/0206_climate1.html. A first-rate overview of the current data and consequences of global warming.

National Oceanic and Atmospheric Administration Web site. Available online. URL: http://www.noaa.gov/. A top-notch resource for news, research, diagrams, and photographs relating to the oceans, coasts, weather, climate, and research.

"Resource Guide, Elementary and Middle School Resources: Physical Parameters." Consortium for Oceanographic Activities for Students and Teachers. Available online. URL: http://www.coast-nopp.org/toc.html. Accessed December 10, 2003. A Web site for students and teachers that includes information and activities.

"Sea Snakes in Australian Waters." CRC Reef Research Centre. Available online. URL: http://www.reef.crc.org.au/discover/plantsanimals/seasnakes. Accessed November 18, 2004. An overview of sea snake classification, breeding, and venom.

U.S. Fish and Wildlife Service Web site. Available online. URL: http://www.fws.gov/. A federal conservation organization that covers a wide range of topics, including fisheries, endangered animals, the condition of the oceans, and conservation news.

Index

Note: *Italic* page numbers indicate illustrations.
  C indicates color insert pages.

139